Heritage Edition

The Iroquois

Indians of North America

Heritage Edition

◀ Indians ▶
▶ of North ◀
◀ America ▶

The Cherokees

The Choctaw

The Comanche

The Hopi

The Iroquois

The Mohawk

The Teton Sioux

Heritage Edition

◀ Indians ▶
of North
◀ America ▶

The
Iroquois

Barbara Graymont

Foreword by
Ada E. Deer
University of Wisconsin-Madison

CHELSEA HOUSE
PUBLISHERS
A Haights Cross Communications ✦ Company

Philadelphia

COVER: An Iroquois carving of the original False Face, Hadui, whose nose is bent and broken.

CHELSEA HOUSE PUBLISHERS

VP, NEW PRODUCT DEVELOPMENT Sally Cheney
DIRECTOR OF PRODUCTION Kim Shinners
CREATIVE MANAGER Takeshi Takahashi
MANUFACTURING MANAGER Diann Grasse

Staff for THE IROQUOIS

EXECUTIVE EDITOR Lee Marcott
EDITOR Christian Green
PRODUCTION EDITOR Noelle Nardone
PHOTO EDITOR Sarah Bloom
SERIES AND COVER DESIGNER Keith Trego
LAYOUT 21st Century Publishing and Communications, Inc.

A Haights Cross Communications ✦ Company

www.chelseahouse.com

First Printing

9 8 7 6 5 4 3 2 1

Library of Congress Cataloging-in-Publication Data

Graymont, Barbara.
  The Iroquois / Barbara Graymont.
    p. cm.—(Indians of North America, revised)
Includes bibliographical references and index.
  ISBN 0-7910-7993-7 — ISBN 0-7910-8351-9 (pbk.)
  1. Iroquois Indians. I. Title. II. Series.
E99.I7G66 2004
974.7004'9755—dc22

                                                    2004004704

Contents

Foreword

Ada E. Deer

American Indians are an integral part of our nation's life and history. Yet most Americans think of their Indian neighbors as stereotypes; they are woefully uninformed about them as fellow humans. They know little about the history, culture, and contributions of Native people. In this new millennium, it is essential for every American to know, understand, and share in our common heritage. The Cherokee teacher, the Mohawk steelworker, and the Ojibwe writer all express their tribal heritage while living in mainstream America.

The revised INDIANS OF NORTH AMERICA series, which focuses on some of the continent's larger tribes, provides the reader with an accurate perspective that will better equip him/her to live and work in today's world. Each tribe has a unique history and culture, and knowledge of individual tribes is essential to understanding the Indian experience.

Prior to the arrival of Columbus in 1492, scholars estimate the Native population north of the Rio Grande ranged from seven to twenty-five million people who spoke more than three hundred different languages. It has been estimated that ninety percent of the Native population was wiped out by disease, war, relocation, and starvation. Today there are more than 567 tribes, which have a total population of more than two million. When Columbus arrived in the Bahamas, the Arawak Indians greeted him with gifts, friendship, and hospitality. He noted their ignorance of guns and swords and wrote they could easily be overtaken with fifty men and made to do whatever he wished. This unresolved clash in perspectives continues to this day.

A holistic view recognizing the connections of all people, the land, and animals pervades the life and thinking of Native people. These core values—respect for each other and all living things; honoring the elders; caring, sharing, and living in balance with nature; and using not abusing the land and its resources— have sustained Native people for thousands of years.

American Indians are recognized in the U.S. Constitution. They are the only group in this country who has a distinctive *political* relationship with the federal government. This relationship is based on the U.S. Constitution, treaties, court decisions, and attorney-general opinions. Through the treaty process, millions of acres of land were ceded *to* the U.S. government *by* the tribes. In return, the United States agreed to provide protection, health care, education, and other services. All 377 treaties were broken by the United States. Yet treaties are the supreme law of the land as stated in the U.S. Constitution and are still valid. Treaties made more than one hundred years ago uphold tribal rights to hunt, fish, and gather.

Since 1778, when the first treaty was signed with the Lenni-Lenape, tribal sovereignty has been recognized and a government-to-government relationship was established. This concept of tribal power and authority has continuously been misunderstood by the general public and undermined by the states. In a series of court decisions in the 1830s, Chief Justice John Marshall described tribes as "domestic dependent nations." This status is not easily understood by most people and is rejected by state governments who often ignore and/or challenge tribal sovereignty. Sadly, many individual Indians and tribal governments do not understand the powers and limitations of tribal sovereignty. An overarching fact is that Congress has plenary, or absolute, power over Indians and can exercise this sweeping power at any time. Thus, sovereignty is tenuous.

Since the July 8, 1970, message President Richard Nixon issued to Congress in which he emphasized "self-determination without termination," tribes have re-emerged and have utilized the opportunities presented by the passage of major legislation such as the American Indian Tribal College Act (1971), Indian Education Act (1972), Indian Education and Self-Determination Act (1975), American Indian Health Care Improvement Act (1976), Indian Child Welfare Act (1978), American Indian Religious Freedom Act (1978), Indian Gaming Regulatory Act (1988), and Native American Graves Preservation and Repatriation Act (1990). Each of these laws has enabled tribes to exercise many facets of their sovereignty and consequently has resulted in many clashes and controversies with the states and the general public. However, tribes now have more access to and can afford attorneys to protect their rights and assets.

Under provisions of these laws, many Indian tribes reclaimed power over their children's education with the establishment of tribal schools and thirty-one tribal colleges. Many Indian children have been rescued from the foster-care system. More tribal people are freely practicing their traditional religions. Tribes with gaming revenue have raised their standard of living with improved housing, schools, health clinics, and other benefits. Ancestors' bones have been reclaimed and properly buried. All of these laws affect and involve the federal, state, and local governments as well as individual citizens.

Tribes are no longer people of the past. They are major players in today's economic and political arenas; contributing millions of dollars to the states under the gaming compacts and supporting political candidates. Each of the tribes in INDIANS OF NORTH AMERICA demonstrates remarkable endurance, strength, and adaptability. They are buying land, teaching their language and culture, and creating and expanding their economic base, while developing their people and making decisions for future generations. Tribes will continue to exist, survive, and thrive.

Ada E. Deer
University of Wisconsin-Madison
June 2004

1

The Time of Troubles

In the land south of Lake Ontario, along the Mohawk River and westward to the Finger Lakes and Genesee River, in what is now New York State, there lived five related but separate Indian *nations*. To the Europeans who would later come into their territory, they would be known as the Mohawk, Oneida, Onondaga, Cayuga, and Seneca. Collectively, the newcomers would refer to these Indians as the *Iroquois*. Each nation lived in its own separate territory, in several villages built in forest clearings and tightly stockaded for protection against attacks from enemies.

To the east, along the Hudson River, were the Mahican, long-time enemies of all the Iroquois people. The Mohawk, the Iroquois tribe whose territory was nearest the Mahican, bore the major burden of this ongoing warfare. Fierce on the warpath, the Mohawk attacked not only the Mahican but also the Abenaki and other New England Indians in the east and the *Algonquian*-speaking *tribes* in the

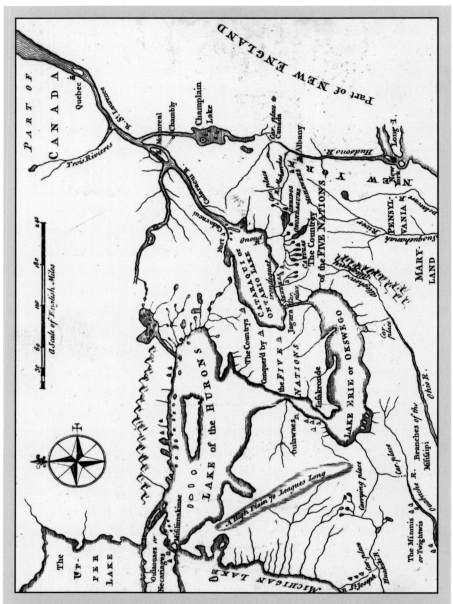

The five nations of the Iroquois—Mohawk, Seneca, Cayuga, Onondaga, and Oneida—lived in what is now New York State, between the Adirondack Mountains in the east and Niagara Falls in the west. However, at its peak, the Iroquois sphere of influence extended south to the Chesapeake Bay, west to the junction of the Mississippi and Ohio Rivers, north to lower Ontario, and east to northern New England.

north. The Mohawks were always feared. They called themselves *Ganiengehaka*, "People of the Place of the Flint," or, as they are generally called, "People of the Flint Country." But so devastating were they in battle that their enemies gave them the name by which they have since become known—*Mowak* (Mohawk)—"Man Eaters."

Warfare was a way of life for all of the Iroquois nations. So often did the sun shine down upon men fighting that it was said in those days that the sun loved war. The power and the prestige of the warriors increased with each battle. They had become so attached to war and the glory it brought them that they could not give it up.

The Iroquois tribes not only made war upon their enemies but, most unfortunately, even on one another. Attacks by a war party of one Iroquois nation upon the village of another would lead to reprisals, revenge, and long years of *blood feud*. Fear and hatred were the normal feelings of each Iroquois nation toward the others. Even in his own village, a warrior could not always trust his neighbor. People used to say that when the clouds were hiding our grandmother the Moon, it was not safe to wander around at night.

The most famous and most feared of these warriors was Tadodaho, a chieftain of the Onondaga Nation. He was intelligent, crafty, and evil. He had the appearance of a cruel and ugly monster, with his hair matted and twisted, like snakes encircling his head. Tadodaho's reputation as a mighty warrior and a powerful wizard attracted a group of young men who followed him, eager to do his bidding. When those who opposed him died mysteriously or were driven away from the village, the Onondaga people became terrified. They whispered among themselves that Tadodaho could destroy people even when he was not present. His strength and cunning, his abilities as a sorcerer, and his reputation for cannibalism effectively silenced those who wished to establish peace among all peoples.

Tadodaho and his warriors intimidated their own Onondaga people and terrorized the nearby Cayuga settlements and the Seneca villages farther west. At night, people had frightful dreams of being tortured and murdered. The whole Iroquois country was fast becoming a wasteland.

Among the Onondaga, there was one courageous leader who had no fear of Tadodaho. The good chief Hayenwatha had frequently tried to reform the evil war leader and straighten his crooked mind. Tadodaho refused to accept the advice or leadership of any man. He regarded Hayenwatha's peacemaking efforts with contempt.

Hayenwatha loved his people more than his own safety. Determined to continue his campaign for peace, he sent messages to all the Onondaga villages, inviting the people to attend a grand council. There, he would present his proposals for mutual peace, friendship, and cooperation. When the appointed day arrived, a large crowd assembled around the council fire. The people waited expectantly. They hoped that the great orator Hayenwatha would give them good news: that the time of troubles would end so they could henceforth live without fear.

As the meeting was about to begin, Tadodaho appeared, angry and ferocious. He said not a word, but his presence cast a shadow over the gathering. The people saw his ruthless warriors scattered throughout the crowd. So great was the fear that those who opposed Tadodaho would be murdered by him or his followers that no one dared debate. The council turned out to be a failure.

Not long afterward, Hayenwatha's eldest daughter became sick and died. Her illness could not be cured by the skill of any healer. People were convinced that her death was the result of Tadodaho's *witchcraft*.

If Hayenwatha had been more cautious or more cowardly, he might have retired to his own home, attended solely to his family affairs, and given up his great plan for peace. But this good man knew that a chief had to be ready to make great sacrifices for the welfare of his nation. Accordingly, he did not hesitate to send runners out again to call the villagers to a second council.

This meeting was no more successful than the first. Fewer people attended and most again shuddered with fear at the presence of Tadodaho and his warrior band. Once more, the people departed with nothing accomplished.

After the second council, the second of Hayenwatha's daughters died in the same manner as her elder sister. Was it a coincidence? Now people were certain that it was Tadodaho's doing, that it was a contest of will and power between two great men—one evil and one good. How long could evil continue to overcome good?

For Hayenwatha, the work of reform was becoming not only difficult but highly dangerous. Only sorrow and more tragedy lay ahead as he tried to carry out his responsibility as a faithful chief. He refused to abandon his struggle, however. After the burial of his second daughter and the end of the period of mourning, he called a third council.

The youngest daughter of Hayenwatha accompanied her father to this council. She was his beloved and his greatest delight—not only was she the only surviving member of his family, but she was soon going to make him a grandfather. As the council delegates began to gather, she went to the edge of the clearing with the other women to help collect firewood for cooking. Busy with her task, she paid little attention to the assembly.

Suddenly, a great eagle appeared, gracefully gliding over the treetops and circling the clearing where the delegates were coming together. Tadodaho was the first to see him. Pointing upward, he cried out to his most skilled warrior to shoot the bird. The man immediately sent an arrow flying from his bowstring and killed the eagle as it flew.

The great bird fell to earth next to Hayenwatha's daughter. With a shout of delight, the warriors rushed forward to pluck the valuable feathers from the fallen eagle. In their haste to claim their prize, they unthinkingly knocked down the helpless young woman and trampled her to death.

The grief-stricken Hayenwatha had now lost the remaining member of his family and was left alone in the world. His most beloved daughter lay dead upon the field, still carrying within her the child who would never be born. As the people gathered around in horror and remorse, Hayenwatha mournfully cried out, "I have now lost all my daughters and in the death of this, my last daughter, you have accidentally and unwittingly killed two beings."

The Iroquois Story of Creation

Long before there were human beings, there were Sky People. They dwelled in the celestial world. In those days, there was no sun. All light came from the large white blossoms on the celestial tree that stood in front of the Lodge of the Sky Chief. This Sky Chief had married a young wife. In time this wife, Sky Woman, began to show signs that she would soon bear a child.

There was a troublesome being, called Firedragon, in the Sky World. Firedragon was always spreading rumors. Now he whispered to Sky Chief that the child who was about to be born would not be his. In a fit of anger and jealousy, Sky Chief uprooted the great celestial tree in front of his lodge. He pushed his wife through the hole where the tree had once stood.

Sky Woman fell rapidly down toward the vast dark waters below. The birds, feeling sorry for her, flew underneath and gently supported her, breaking her fall and carrying her slowly downward. At the same time, the water animals hurried to make a place for her. Turtle said that he would support a world on his back. The sea animals plunged down into the water looking for some earth. Muskrat succeeded and came up with a large mouthful of earth, which he placed on Turtle's back. The light from the blossoms of the fallen celestial tree shone through the hole where it had stood and became the sun. When Sky Woman landed, everything was in readiness for her, with grass and trees beginning to grow.

Having met only frustration and despair in trying to bring peace to his people, Hayenwatha left his Onondaga village. Overcome with grief and rage, he plunged into the forest and became a lonely wanderer. On his long and sorrowful journey, his grief began more and more to distort his mind.

Completely alone and constantly grieving, he felt that goodness had left him and that he had taken on the characteristics of Tadodaho, his adversary. His face, once kindly, now grew dismal and frightening. In the depths of his depression, he became convinced that he was a cannibal. His mind was no longer straight. In his enormous grief, it had become crooked.

Sky Woman gave birth to a daughter. When this daughter grew to womanhood, she, too, became pregnant. No one knows whether her husband was Turtle or West Wind, but she gave birth to two remarkable twin boys—one good and one evil. The Good Twin was born in the usual way. But the Evil Twin was in a hurry and pushed through his mother's side to be born. In doing so, he killed his mother.

Sky Woman buried her daughter, and plants miraculously began to grow from various parts of the daughter's body—a tobacco plant, a cornstalk, a bean bush, and a squash vine. This was the origin of all the plants that would be most important to the human beings who would come later.

The Good Twin and the Evil Twin quickly grew to manhood. As soon as they were grown, they proved true to their names. The Good Twin began to create all sorts of good things: plants, animals, medicinal herbs, rivers, and streams. The Evil Twin began to spoil his brother's work, putting rapids and boulders in the rivers, creating poisonous plants, thorns and briars, diseases, and monsters. The Good and Evil Twins fought against each other to see who would predominate in creation, but the Evil could never overcome the Good. Finally, the Good Twin created human beings to enjoy all the good things he had made for them. And that is how it all began.

The bald eagle, one of the Iroquois' national symbols, plays a prominent part in Iroquois myth and lore. According to legend, the bird soared from the heavens to protect the union of five Iroquois states when the Iroquois Confederacy was founded more than five hundred years ago.

On the pathway of sorrow he had only nature for a companion. No fellow human ever came to lift his burden from him. It was to nature that he began to look for relief.

One morning, as he wandered on his way, he saw a stand of rushes growing before him. He cut a quantity of the jointed rushes and strung them together into three strings of beads. Then he cut two forked sticks and thrust their long ends into the ground. He placed a pole across the forked angle of the sticks and sat down before them. Then he placed his three strings over the pole and said to himself: "This would I do if I found anyone burdened with grief even as I am. I would console them for they would be covered with night and wrapped in darkness. This would I lift with words of condolence and these strings of beads would become words with which I would address them."

This, the later Iroquois would say, was the origin of the condolence ritual, by which mourners even today are comforted and relieved of their sorrow. As Hayenwatha turned eastward in his journey, he came to an area of small lakes. On the shores he saw numerous small white shells. He picked them up and strung them together. Then he put the several strings of white shells around his neck as a sign of peace, for he was entering the land of the Mohawk, the People of the Flint Country.

When he reached the edge of the forest on the outskirts of one of the Mohawk villages, he sat down on the stump of a fallen tree. Soon a young woman came out of the village carrying an elm-bark bucket to get water from a nearby spring. When she saw Hayenwatha sitting there quietly, she returned to her village and related the news: "A man, or a figure like a man, is seated by the spring, having his breast covered with strings of white shells."

At this time a man from the north, Deganawidah, was living in the village. He had come to the Mohawks with a message of peace. He knew that the stranger came as a friend, for the white shells were emblems of peace. He therefore sent a messenger to welcome Hayenwatha and escort him into the village.

As Hayenwatha accompanied his escort into the village of long bark-covered lodges, he felt friendship all around him. These Mohawks, so feared by their enemies, lived among themselves in a kindly manner. The escort took the visitor to the lodge of Deganawidah, who rose to greet Hayenwatha. Even before they spoke, the two men understood each other.

"My younger brother," said Deganawidah, "I perceive you have suffered from some deep grief. You are a chief among your people and yet you are wandering about."

Hayenwatha told his host of his great sorrow in the loss of his entire family and related to him the bitter experience of his wandering and his loneliness.

"Dwell here with me. I will represent your sorrow to the people who live here," Deganawidah assured him.

As he promised, Deganawidah laid all the sad troubles he had heard before the chiefs in council. Their hearts were touched, and they sent Deganawidah to lift their guest's burden.

When Deganawidah returned to his lodge, he heard Hayenwatha mourning before the three strings of beads on the pole before him. He thereupon approached his new friend and took up the strings to condole with him.

Presenting the first string, Deganawidah said, "When a person has suffered a great loss caused by death and is grieving, the tears blind his eyes so that he cannot see. With these words, I wipe away the tears from your eyes so that now you may see clearly."

Presenting the second string, he said, "When a person has suffered a great loss caused by death and is grieving, there is an obstruction in his ears and he cannot hear. With these words, I remove the obstruction from your ears so that you may once again have perfect hearing."

Presenting the third string, he said, "When a person has suffered a great loss caused by death, his throat is stopped and he cannot speak. With these words, I remove the obstruction from your throat so that you may speak and breathe freely."

These are the basic "three words" of the condolence ceremony, observed by the Iroquois even to this day.

With this ceremony, Hayenwatha's mind became straight once again. He looked upon Deganawidah and thought he had never seen such goodness and kindness before. Surely, he felt, the Master of Life must have led him to this place and to this man.

In turn, Deganawidah saw in Hayenwatha a strong and righteous man, with many talents and abundant courage. He had been searching for such a companion to help him in his mission of peace. Together they could spread the Good News to all the nations.

Here among the People of the Flint Country, Hayenwatha found a new home, a new life, and a great work.

2

The Great Peace

Deganawidah had also been a lonely wanderer before coming to the Mohawk village. He had been born in the land of the Wendot people, a tribe north of Lake Ontario. These people, whom the French would later call the Hurons, were distantly related to the Iroquois tribes south of the lake. Their way of life was similar, even though they spoke a slightly different language. Like the Iroquois, the Wendots honored their women, especially women who had borne children. Among both peoples it was the mothers who chose the chiefs and the mothers who could remove the chiefs from office if they failed in their duties. Every child belonged to the family line of his or her mother.

The women tended to the household duties and did the farming. They raised huge quantities of corn, beans, and squash, which composed the main food supply of the *Iroquoian* people. Together this triad of vegetables was known as "Our Supporters" or "The Three Sisters."

All Iroquois men were hunters and warriors, supplementing the food supply and protecting the villages from attack. Since ancient times, the Wendots had made war against neighboring tribes and especially against their distant kin, the Iroquois who lived south of Lake Ontario. Every young man was expected to do his duty as a warrior and protector of his people.

Young Wendot boys played at war to sharpen the skills they would need later in life, but as he was growing to manhood, Deganawidah talked only of peace, friendship, and unity. This handsome young man was always strictly honest and always spoke with a straight tongue. To the Wendots, however, he was strange. He had departed from the way the Wendots believed a young man should go, and his talk was considered foolishness. Most people believed that the only way to have peace was to smash all enemies, to attack and destroy them before they destroyed you. The grown men regularly went off on war expeditions. The Wendots were of one mind that Deganawidah was not accepting his proper role as a man among them. Furthermore, although he held no office in his nation, he gave people advice on how to live and how to govern, which caused resentment and jealousy. Moreover, he claimed that his message of peace had come to him directly from the Master of Life.

Deganawidah's ideas and actions were noticeably separating him from his people. The Wendots could not understand a man who loved peace more than war. They could not tolerate someone whom they had known since childhood presenting himself to them as a prophet. So great was their animosity toward him that Deganawidah at last came to feel that his message would be better received by other people, far from his home.

After he came to this decision, Deganawidah built a canoe and fondly took leave of his mother and grandmother. He told them that it was time for him to depart and search out the council smoke of far-flung nations in order to preach his message of peace. "It is my business," he told them, "to stop the shedding of blood among human beings."

He then set out on Lake Ontario, paddling south toward the far shore to the land of the five Iroquois nations. When he reached his destination, he saw some men along the shore running to him. When they came close, he asked what they were doing in that lonely place. They replied that they were hunters far from their own village because of troubles at home. Deganawidah directed them to go back to their village and announce to their chief that the Great Peace had come and that their village would now be free of troubles. "And if he asks you from whence came the Good Tidings of Peace and Power," Deganawidah continued, "you will say that the Messenger of the Good Tidings of Peace and Power will come in a few days." When they asked him his name, Deganawidah responded, "It is I who came from the west and am going eastward and am called Deganawidah in the world."

As he had instructed them, the hunters returned to their village to announce to their chief that the Good News of Peace and Power had come. They related their meeting with Deganawidah and said that he would soon arrive at their settlement. The chief expressed great pleasure and satisfaction at the news, for his village had long been troubled.

On his way toward the hunters' settlement, Deganawidah stopped at the small bark lodge of a woman who lived alongside the warriors' path that ran from east to west. It was her custom to greet and feed the warriors whenever they passed by her house on their errands of destruction. She also greeted and fed Deganawidah.

After eating, Deganawidah explained to her the Good News of Peace and Power: "I carry the Mind of the Master of Life and my message will bring an end to the wars between east and west." He instructed her that henceforth she must cease feeding the warriors: "The Word that I bring is that all peoples shall love one another and live together in peace."

"That is indeed a good message," the woman responded. "I take hold of it. I embrace it."

This woman became the first person to accept the Great Peace. Deganawidah therefore named her *Jigonsasee,* or "New Face," because she reflected the New Mind. He appointed her to be the Mother of Nations, the Great Peace Woman, and told her, "I now charge you that you shall be the custodian of the Good Tidings of Peace and Power, so that the human race may live in peace in the future."

Deganawidah then continued on his journey eastward toward the Flint Country, and made his way to one of the Mohawk villages. There, he sat down at the edge of the forest and began to smoke his pipe. This was the custom for a visitor approaching a strange village, so he would not startle the people, who might otherwise mistake him for an enemy.

When men from the village came to question him, he explained that he was on a mission of peace and so they took him to their chiefs. After presenting his peace message to the chiefs, he offered it to all the people of the village. The Mohawks had suffered greatly from war and welcomed this proposal for friendship, which would mean unity and justice among all peoples.

Among the Iroquois tribes, the code of honor required revenge for a life taken. Killing always led to more killing, and the cycle of revenge thus meant perpetual war. If one tribe had proposed peace to another, it would have been considered cowardice and weakness. There seemed to be no way out of this bloody dilemma.

Now this tribeless man, Deganawidah, had come to the Mohawks with a plan to end their troubles. Because he had no tribe of his own, he was neutral. He had never been involved in any of the killing. Because no man's hand was against him, he could become a peace messenger among the tribes without disgrace or accusation of cowardice. The Mohawks therefore gladly took hold of his message and became the first nation to accept the Great Peace.

It was after Deganawidah had prepared the minds of the People of the Flint Country for the Good News that Hayenwatha arrived and was condoled by Deganawidah. After his mind had become straight, Hayenwatha was accepted into the Mohawk Nation and became one of its chiefs. In their different ways, each of these two men had tried to promote peace. Now they joined together to strengthen their work and spread the message of peace far beyond their village.

What they proposed was the formation of a confederation, or family, of nations. Each tribe that accepted the Good News of Peace and Power would become a nation within the confederation. Together they would be known as the League of the Iroquois. To design the government for the confederation, they drew on a structure that was already familiar to them. The league would become an extended family, based on the local kinship groups known as *clans*.

The most basic unit of Iroquois society was a group of relatives who traced its descent from a single woman. In the Mohawk language, this group was called the *ohwachira*. The eldest woman of each ohwachira was generally its head. Two or more ohwachiras made up a clan, and everyone in a clan considered every other clan member to be a relative. Because of this relationship, marriage within a clan was forbidden. Occasionally, a clan had only one ohwachira, usually because the other ohwachiras in that clan had died out.

A person was born into his or her clan, inheriting the family and clan affiliation of his or her mother. A stranger like Deganawidah or Hayenwatha, or a war captive, could be incorporated into the tribe by adoption. Adoptees would take on the identity of the family and clan that adopted them and thereby become full-fledged members of the tribe. Adoption was the Iroquois method of conferring citizenship.

Each clan had as its name and symbol a certain bird or animal. The Mohawk and the Oneida had only three clans: Turtle, Wolf, and Bear. These three clans were also present among the Onondaga, Cayuga, and Seneca; but these three tribes had other clans as well, such as Snipe, Heron, Beaver, Deer, Eel, and Hawk. Each clan was entitled to a certain number of chiefs, and the head mothers of the ohwachiras chose the chiefs for their own particular clan. Each clan governed itself and also joined with the other clans in governing the village and the tribe. (For additional information on these family groups, enter "Indian clans" into any search engine and browse the many sites listed.)

It was this clan government that Deganawidah and Hayenwatha planned to apply to the whole confederacy they hoped to establish. The clan chiefs would become the confederacy chiefs, but the government of the confederation would not interfere with the independence of the clan or tribal governments.

The Great Peace, or *Kayanernh-kowa,* that Deganawidah and Hayenwatha established would have three parts, each with a double meaning:

The Good Word, which is righteousness in action, bringing justice for all.

Health, which is a sound mind in a sound body, bringing peace on Earth.

Power, which is the establishment of civil authority, bringing with it the increase in spiritual power in keeping with the will of the Master of Life.

After the Mohawks accepted the plan of the confederacy, they directed Deganawidah and Hayenwatha to send messengers to their neighbors to the immediate west, the Oneidas, the People of the Standing Stone. There, the messengers were to lay the proposal before the leading chief, Odatshedeh.

After he listened to the messengers' explanation of the Great Peace, Odatshedeh replied, "I will consider this plan and answer you tomorrow."

The messengers immediately understood that "tomorrow" meant "next year," for the Iroquois always gave long and serious consideration to every important proposal.

After a year had passed, the Oneida council sent word that they would take hold of the Great Peace. A treaty was therefore concluded between the Oneidas and the Mohawks, which laid the foundation of the League of Peace.

The next people to the west were the Onondagas. They were willing to accept the offer of Deganawidah and Hayenwatha, but their powerful chief Tadodaho refused. Despite this setback, the delegation journeyed on to the next nation, the Cayugas.

When the Cayugas heard of the proposal for peace, unity, and power, they accepted the offer with great relief. For many years, they had suffered from the attacks of the powerful Onondagas. Now they felt the strength and security the League of Peace would give them. The ambassadors then proceeded farther west to the Genesee River and the land of the Senecas, the People of the Great Hill. Here, too, they would have a problem. Various factions among the Senecas prevented the nation from reaching a unanimous decision.

The Seneca chiefs replied to Deganawidah: "We lords on either side of the river have decided to accept your message which you left. The only difficulty which we have now to contend with is that our chief warrior and his deputy have failed to agree with us to accept the message, and they have the power to control the people, and we lords on either side of the river are totally bewildered and fail to see a way out of the difficulty."

Deganawidah encouraged the Senecas to settle their problems, and he accepted those chiefs who had grasped the Good News. With the confederacy growing stronger with every passing year, he was confident that a way would soon be found to persuade the unwilling portion of the Senecas to join the movement for unity.

Then Deganawidah and Hayenwatha turned their attentions back to the Onondagas, where Tadodaho remained coldly opposed to the confederation. They were determined to win the reluctant chief over through a combination of spiritual power, a curing ceremony, and political persuasion.

A delegation from the newly formed League went to the Onondagas, with a singer in front singing a peace hymn and other sacred songs that Deganawidah had taught. The Onondaga chiefs welcomed them and took them to the lodge of Tadodaho. There, Deganawidah sang the peace hymn before the evil-minded chieftain and, after he had finished, he rubbed down Tadodaho's body in a sacred medicine ceremony. All Iroquois, even those who were antisocial or malicious, believed in the reality of the supernatural and in the power of medicine ceremonies to cure the mind and the body. The people watched closely to see if the sacred herbs and the ritual would produce the desired effect on their chief.

Deganawidah then explained to Tadodaho that the assembled people represented all the nations united in a strong league, but that they wished to lay their heads before him. It was a metaphor for submission, meaning that they would all recognize him as their leading chief. Tadodaho was silent.

Another chief then spoke, relaying the opinions of the chiefs, warriors, and the Peace Woman, Jigonsasee, who were present: "The lords and all the chief warriors and this great woman, our mother, have all agreed to submit the Good Tidings of Peace and Power to you, and thus if you approve and confirm the message, you will have the power and be the Fire-Keeper of our Confederate Council, and the smoke from it will rise and pierce the sky, and all the nations will be subject to you."

Then Tadodaho broke his silence and said, "It is well. I will now answer the mission which brought you here. I now truly

Hayenwatha and Deganawidah, the great peacemaker, were determined to unite the Iroquois people into a confederation. Standing in their way of achieving the Great Peace, or *Kayanernh-kowa* was Tadodaho (right), a chieftain of the Onondaga Nation. This drawing depicts Hayenwatha's and Deganawidah's meeting with the great sorcerer, who had the appearance of a cruel and ugly monster. Hayenwatha and Deganawidah eventually won over Tadodaho after they cured his body and mind through a sacred medicine ceremony.

confirm and accept your message, the object of which brought you here."

Tadodaho's mind had now been made straight.

It still remained to convince that portion of the Seneca Nation who followed war chiefs to come into the League. This was accomplished when the confederate chiefs and warriors unanimously decided to make the two Seneca war chiefs the war captains of the confederacy, to lead the Five Nations in case of attack and to command the defense of the confederacy. The Seneca war chiefs accepted this offer and Deganawidah pronounced the power of the League to be "full and complete."

Deganawidah chose as a symbol of the League of the Five Nations the pine tree, the Tree of the Great Long Leaves. The tree had four symbolic roots, the Great White Roots of Peace, spreading north, east, south, and west. If any other nation ever wished to join the League, it would have to follow the White Roots of Peace to the source and take shelter beneath the tree. Atop the tree, he placed an eagle to scream out a warning at the approach of danger. He symbolically planted the tree in the land of the Onondagas, the place of the Great Council Fire. There, the confederate lords, or peace chiefs, would sit beneath it and be caretakers of the Great Peace. And these lords, the chiefs, would figuratively never die, because their chiefly titles would be passed down to their successors forever. In this way, the League of the Five Nations would always be kept alive.

How a Legend Was Made

In the mid-nineteenth century, Henry Rowe Schoolcraft, a government agent among the Indians of the Upper Great Lakes, began to write down the folklore and legends of the Ojibwa Indians, including the tale of the demigod Nanabozho. He also began to collect material for his 1846 book, *Notes on the Iroquois*, and acquired from the New York author J. V. H. Clark stories relating to Chief Hayenwatha, or Hiawatha, as the name was sometimes written. In ignorance, Schoolcraft applied the name of the Iroquois chief to Nanabozho and published the result in *The Hiawatha Legends*. The poet Henry Wadsworth Longfellow became acquainted with Schoolcraft's writings and was inspired to compose a long poem about the exploits of Nanabozho and his companions under the mistaken impression that he was writing about a hero named Hiawatha. Longfellow's fanciful poem, "The Song of Hiawatha," though a moving and beautiful literary creation, had nothing whatsoever to do with the noted Iroquois chieftain and only served to obscure and confuse this leader's very great achievements.

The Iroquois also referred to the Great Peace, or the confederacy, as the Extended Lodge, or *Kanonghsionni* in the Mohawk language. The name was a reference to the long, bark-covered lodges in which multiple related families lived in their villages. This family lodge now figuratively became even longer, or extended, so that it covered the entire country of the Five Nations, binding all its inhabitants together as one family.

After completing his work, Deganawidah instructed the people never to pass his name down to another and never to speak it again except in ritual use or when the Great Peace was being discussed. Accordingly, out of respect, Deganawidah in later years was generally referred to by Iroquois speakers as "The Man from the North" or "The Peacemaker." The names of all the other founding chiefs, including that of Hayenwatha, would be inherited by their successors in their respective clans.

No one today knows exactly when the Confederacy of the Five Nations was founded. We know only that when the Europeans first met the Iroquois, their confederacy was already very old. The seventeenth-century *Jesuit* missionaries referred to the League of the Five Nations as "ancient." Horatio Hale, a nineteenth-century scholar who gave the subject much study, put the date of the founding at approximately A.D. 1459.

The history of the League's founding had been handed down orally among the Iroquois for hundreds of years. After several nineteenth-century non-Indian scholars such as Horatio Hale and Lewis Henry Morgan began to publish articles and books about Iroquois history, ritual, and *culture*, a number of knowledgeable Iroquois themselves undertook to write down the story of the origin of the League. Each person who told the story, however, told it in a different way. There were many versions and no two accounts agreed about every detail or even about the order of events. As the tale had been recounted in every village year after year, over a period of perhaps five hundred years, fact had become mixed with legend. This transformation of the historical account shows the extent to which these events had taken on a sacred character for the Iroquois. The exact details were not nearly as important to them as testifying to the authenticity of their confederacy and the significance of what their ancestors had done for them. In establishing unity and preserving their nationhood, the ancestors had provided for all time a purpose and a way of life for the people of the Extended Lodge.

3

The Extended Lodge Flourishes

The establishment of the League of the Five Nations strengthened and protected them from enemies on the outside and ensured their ongoing peaceful coexistence within. They shared their hunting grounds with one another and the men hunted in peace. The women tilled the fields around their villages and planted crops, confident that any enemies were too far away to disturb their homeland.

The Creator had given them the Three Sisters, Our Supporters—corn, beans, and squash. First they planted the corn in the fields in small hills about three feet apart, row upon row. When the young corn plants came up, the women planted bean or squash seeds in the same hills. These crops, which came up later, would twine around the cornstalks. This method of planting, which kept the bean and squash vines off the ground, made it easy to hoe the weeds and harvest the crops. When the soil around a village became exhausted, usually in ten to fifteen years, the people moved to a more promising site. After the initial effort of rebuilding their homes and clearing and tilling the fields, they adjusted easily to the new locale.

For the Iroquois, as for tribal people generally, religion was an inseparable part of daily life. Spiritual powers were everywhere in the natural world, and people always sought to keep in the right relationship to them. The Iroquois were grateful to the Creator and the benevolent supernatural beings for their help. Knowledge of how to perform the proper rituals and ward off evil forces was essential. In every season of the year, great ceremonies were held to give thanks for the bounties of nature. These occasions unified the community in a common purpose and way of life.

One of the oldest of the agricultural observances was the Green Corn Festival, held at the time the corn, beans, and squashes became ripe, when the people rejoiced and gave thanks for their good fortune. In later years, when agriculture became even more prominent in their lives, the Iroquois developed a cycle of agricultural thanksgiving ceremonials. At planting time and as the various berries and crop plants ripened, from the time the maple sap flowed in early spring to the final gathering of the crops in late fall, there was a joyous round of thanksgiving services. A ritual leader recited thanksgiving chants, the people performed religious dances to the accompaniment of rattle or drum, and the entire community feasted to mark all these observances.

In winter, after the men returned from the fall hunt, the Iroquois held their great New Year's or Midwinter Festival, called "The Most Excellent Faith" in their language. This was a time of renewal and cleansing—a cleansing of people's spirits and a ritual cleansing of their homes. On the opening day, the elders who were the keepers of the faith went to every home in the village to announce the beginning of the festival. They instructed all residents to clean their homes, visit their neighbors, and stir the ashes on their hearths. Then the people went around the village with small paddles, visiting their neighbors and stirring the ashes in each home. The faithkeepers also visited homes to stir the ashes and give thanks to the Creator for preserving the people through the year. There is evidence that at one time the people extinguished the old fires in their homes and kindled new ones as a symbol of renewal. In more recent times, the new-fire rite has fallen into disuse and only the ash-stirring rite continues.

An essential part of the Midwinter Festival was the practice of dream guessing. The Iroquois regarded dreams as important communications from supernatural beings. For this reason, it was necessary that any instructions given in a dream be followed. People who had a dream to be guessed would describe it in a disguised fashion, requiring their neighbors to guess the actual content, and then the neighbors had to satisfy the dreamer's desires. With satisfaction received, the troubled minds of the dreamers were restored to wholeness.

Two Jesuit missionaries who witnessed the Midwinter Festival at Onondaga in 1656 described the ceremony. Some of the dreamers who came into their cabins behaved in a most extreme manner—singing, shouting, dancing, and threatening— demanding that their dreams be guessed and satisfied. Others were more subdued in their requests. Among the latter was a woman who came in and quietly laid down a mattock, or

Prayer Recited During the Midwinter Festival

I am thankful that I am alive in health. Now the time has come in which the Midwinter Ceremony is marked. So then now do you, Sky-Holder who live in the sky, do you continue to listen? . . . You next, the nocturnal Orb of Light, our Grandmother, and now also the Stars on the sky in many places, do you know that every one of those who remain alive has made preparation to thank you now with one voice? Now, our Grandmother, they thank you, and also the stars fixed on the sky in many places.

digging hoe. The people guessed that she was asking for a plot of land. "That was just what she had in mind," reported the Jesuits, "and she was satisfied with five furrows for planting Indian corn."

In assessing the importance of this dream-guessing ceremony for the community, the Jesuits explained: "It would be cruelty and a sort of murder not to give a man what his dream called for, for the refusal might cause his death. Therefore they may see themselves stripped of their all without any hope of recompense. For whatever they give is never returned to them, unless they dream it themselves, or pretend to dream it. In general, they are too scrupulous to make such a pretense, which would, as they suppose, cause all sorts of misfortunes."

To the Jesuits, the entire ceremony was offensive and foolish; but they apparently understood its deep significance to the Iroquois. This dream guessing served a major purpose of releasing tension in the community. Long before the development of the modern science of psychology, the Iroquois recognized that illness could be caused by the mind as well as by natural forces (such as injuries) or by witchcraft. Disorders of the mind were, they believed, often caused by unconscious desires, which might be revealed to a person in a dream. To make the ill person well again, it was essential for a wish-dream to be fulfilled, either actually or symbolically. A dream of hostility against a member of the community was always fulfilled symbolically rather than in actuality. In this way, the peace and unity of the village were preserved and the dreamer was satisfied.

Modern psychotherapy, drawing on methods developed just a century ago, makes use of dreams as an aid in revealing unconscious desires and emotional problems. According to anthropologist Anthony F. C. Wallace, who studied the Iroquois wish-dreams in the 1950s, the Iroquois achieved "a great deal of psychological sophistication" in making this discovery independently and several centuries earlier.

In the wintertime, after the earth had died and when the spirits that guarded the growing things were asleep, the people liked to sit around their fires and tell ghost stories and tales of the supernaturals. One favorite story was of the carnivorous (meat-eating) skeleton who chased lonely travelers at night in order to eat them. One could sometimes hear this fiend's hollow moan in the stillness of the night. There were also stories of flying heads—bodiless creatures who were big and frightful and darted rapidly through the air with their long hair streaming around them. Other tales told of the exploits of a race of stone giants, the most feared of all monsters, who used to wander about the countryside in olden days doing evil and even eating people.

The storytellers also fascinated their listeners with accounts of the Naked Bear and the warrior who overcame him, of the Great Horned Serpent, the Monster Mosquito, witches, and talking animals. There was no end to these marvelous tales of terror, wonder, and courage. The folklore of the Iroquois people was part of their children's traditional education. They learned all the stories at an early age and, in later years, would pass them down to their own children and grandchildren. (For additional information on these stories, enter "Iroquois myths" into any search engine and browse the many sites listed.)

The supernatural world was also very near when healing arts were practiced. Physical illness, the Iroquois believed, could be caused not only by natural means but also by witchcraft and evil spirits. Different types of healers were necessary to treat these various diseases, although a particular medicine man or woman might use several methods of treatment. Herbalists and surgeons used natural remedies to treat the natural causes of their patients' disorders. They treated familiar maladies such as coughs, fevers, ague (severe fever or chill), rattlesnake bites, wounds, and broken bones by probing and cleaning the wounds, setting the bones, and using salves, emetics, or other medicines that they had made themselves, as the situation demanded. They had considerable skill and

Stone giants were some of the most feared supernatural creatures in Iroquois lore. They traveled around the countryside tormenting people and neither arrows nor spears could penetrate their skin. This soapstone carving, titled Stone Giant Emerging, was sculpted by Joseph Jacobs, a Cayuga living on the Tuscarora Reservation.

remarkable knowledge of the healing properties of a vast number of plants.

The conjurers, as the Europeans later called them, attempted to cure through the use of magic arts, by singing ritual medicine songs or incantations to counteract witchcraft and by blowing and sucking over the affected part of a patient's body. Healers who used this latter technique would withdraw from their mouths a hair, splinter, stone, or some other object that they claimed to have sucked out of the sick person's body and announce that this was the cause of the illness. Everyone assumed that the patient had been under the spell of some witch and was now relieved by the healer's counter-magic, as evidenced by removal from the patient's body of a foreign object placed there by the witch. This type of *exorcism* usually had a beneficial psychological effect upon the patient, as well as on members of his or her family.

Other healers had special power to counteract the work of those evil supernaturals who sought to harm humans and spread discord and chaos in the world. For lack of a more precise term in our own language, we refer to them as *shamans*, or priests.

Some healers combined all these skills. Even herbalists believed in the power of magic and would often use it in combination with natural remedies when treating patients. Those who were skilled in the mysteries of medicine were believed to possess sacred knowledge.

From ancient times, the Iroquois had had medicine societies, composed of healers and those who had been cured by the ceremonies of the members. There might be several such societies, each having its own rituals and cures, in any village. When members of some of these medicine societies performed their curing ceremonies, they might wear masks portraying various supernaturals. The masks represented sacred power and were held in high esteem by the Iroquois.

The most important Iroquois ritual commemorates the formation of the confederation, the Good News of Peace and Power. The memory of this great episode, the central event of Iroquois history, is preserved in the Condolence Council. This ritual takes place after a chief dies, when his successor, chosen by the head women of the clan, is raised to chiefly office as a lord of the confederacy. The condolence for a chief, which is still carried on by the Iroquois today, is far more elaborate than the family condolence for a person of lesser rank. This great ceremony is a confederacy-wide event and includes a recitation of the chiefly names of all the earliest lords of the confederacy. The titles exist and are still in use to this day. Their recitation means that the confederacy and its leadership will always remain intact. The Condolence Council is a eulogy to those whose wisdom and energy established the League, a ceremony of comfort for mourners from the family and clan of the deceased, a ritual to replace the one who has died, and a means of ensuring for all time the continuance of the work of the Founding Fathers.

In this ceremony, the antlers of a buck deer are placed upon the head of the new chief as the symbol of his office and power. According to tradition, Deganawidah had explained the practice in the following words: "The reason why we do this is because all people live upon the flesh of the deer, and the reason that we take the emblem of the deer horns is that this institution, the Great Peace, shall be the means of protecting our children hereafter."

As with all peoples who had no writing system, the Iroquois depended upon memory and the spoken word to preserve and pass down their history, traditions, and rituals. This required prodigious feats of memory, for many of the major legends were extremely lengthy, running to seventy-five thousand words or more. The ritualists and archivists of the Five Nations who possessed this large store of essential knowledge were the intellectuals of their communities, equivalent in status to any learned European priest and professor.

As an aid to memory, the Iroquois in later years used shells and shell beads. The Europeans called the beads *wampum*, from *wampumpeag*, a word used by Indians in the area who spoke Algonquian languages. According to the Iroquois tradition, Hayenwatha was the originator of wampum, but archaeological evidence shows that shell beads were in widespread use by the Iroquois and other Indians long before the formation of the Five Nations Confederacy.

However, the more elaborate wampum "belts," with figures or designs on them, made for use in treaty negotiations and as historical records, seem to have been a later development among the Iroquois.

The type of wampum most commonly used in historic times was bead wampum. It was laboriously cut from various seashells, ground and polished, and then bored through the center with a small hand drill. Most wampum was made from the *quahog,* or large hard-shell clam. The Indians of Long Island, in southern New York, were the chief producers of wampum and paid huge quantities of it in tribute, showing that they accepted the superior power of the Iroquois.

The Iroquois strung the beads and wove them into broad multirowed straps or belts for use in various ceremonies and in diplomacy. Strings of mourning wampum were used in condolence ceremonies to remove the grief from those who had lost a family member. Chiefs possessed wampum as a sign of their office. Strings and belts of wampum were used to convey messages in diplomatic relations and to represent the articles of treaties. A messenger who did not present wampum as a pledge of the truth of his words would not be taken seriously. Belts were also used to record great events in Iroquois history. The beads, purple and white, were arranged in designs to represent the event the belt was commemorating.

Certain elders were designated to memorize the various events and treaty articles that the belts represented. Those men could "read" the belts and reproduce their contents with great accuracy. These important belts were stored at Onondaga, the capital of the confederacy, in the care of a designated wampum keeper.

Life was good to the people of the Five Nations for generations after the formation of the confederation. They continued to prosper and generally to enjoy the blessings of nature. Nature was generous and the people were industrious. Iroquois culture was vigorous and dynamic.

The confederacy was a remarkable creation, formed by an early people, showing their great political and social sophistication. They were kindly and reverent, affectionate and loyal toward their families, considerate and tender toward their friends. They had provided within their League a means for extending the house and admitting other peoples into their peaceful way of life. In later years, other Indian tribes would accept this offer and take shelter beneath the Tree of the Great Long Leaves. The Five Nations prospered as a result of their unity. Unfortunately, the surrounding nations did not also benefit from the Great Peace. The Iroquois felt no security on their borders when neighboring nations rejected the confederacy or thwarted their interests. Even after the formation of the League, intermittent raids on the fringes of its borders continued. In later years, these conflicts often became intense beyond belief as the League sought to extend its peace by means of warfare.

4

Iroquois and Europeans

People everywhere aspire to an ideal but must daily deal with realities. So it was with the Iroquois. The ideal was that the Great Peace should extend to all humanity. The reality was that it had to be a peace on Iroquois terms, within the confines of their political and social structure. Because the surrounding peoples did not all agree to this, warfare would continue, the killing of enemies would continue, grief would continue, and retaliation would continue in order to dry the tears of the mourners.

The formation of the League had settled the problem of blood feuds among the five tribes and had brought a general peace to their territory. The issue of how to handle murders or accidental killings of Iroquois by other confederacy members was now to be resolved by the murderer or his family giving gifts, particularly wampum, to the victim's relatives. As a result of this solution, the incessant retaliatory feuds would cease and the people of the confederacy would live together in a spirit of friendship and cooperation.

There were some problems, however, that the establishment of the Great Peace did not solve. Hostilities within the group were now unacceptable and so aggressions had to be directed outward. Warfare was one of the major means by which the men, and particularly young men, achieved fame, prestige, and power. Hunting and fishing, also male occupations, likewise brought prestige but could take place only at certain seasons of the year. Moreover, the women, who were the farmers and gatherers of nuts and wild berries, supplied a large amount of the food. Thus, they shared in the prestige of being nurturers of the village. At certain periods during the year, there was little for the men to do in times of peace. A man's advancement within his community depended upon his skills and achievements, and the successes of the warrior upon the field of battle assured for him the admiration and gratitude of his village. Warriors also served an important social function in bringing back captives to be adopted to replace dead relatives or sacrificed to please certain supernatural beings. One of these supernaturals, Agreskwe, required a gift of the first fruits of the hunting and fishing seasons and the first enemy warriors captured each year.

Continued warfare thus met an important social and religious need among the Iroquois, even after the founding of the League of Peace. The League, in fact, now made it possible for the Five Nations to direct their energies outward against their neighbors not only in defensive wars but, after the coming of the Europeans, in a long series of conquests of neighboring peoples that led to almost perpetual war in the seventeenth and eighteenth centuries.

The object of traditional Indian warfare had been largely to achieve prestige, seek revenge, plunder, or take captives, with the least loss of life to the attacking party as possible. Originally, Indian warfare was not conducted with the severe intensity of

European wars. Objectives were often limited. Indians, including the Iroquois, considered it foolish to fight gloriously to the last man if their war parties could successfully withdraw from a raid or battle and live to fight another day. Early European observers of Indian campaigns, misunderstanding their nature, described them as more sport than serious conflict.

The coming of the Europeans profoundly changed the nature of Iroquois warfare. An economic motive now became predominant as tribes competed for hunting territories and supplies of beaver skins to trade for the European goods that were rapidly becoming important in their lives.

In 1534, Jacques Cartier and his band of French explorers came to Canada and journeyed along the St. Lawrence River on the first of three voyages to that region. First, the French encountered some Algonquian-speaking Indians, then farther upriver, some villages of presently unidentifiable Iroquoian speakers. By the early seventeenth century, these St. Lawrence Iroquois had totally disappeared. Cartier and his men established trade relations with the Indians who lived along the river and entered into friendly alliances with the Algonquian-speaking Indians of that area, particularly the *Algonquin* and Montagnais Nations who lived north and west of the St. Lawrence River. Some French trade goods began to reach other tribes through regular Indian trade networks and through enemy raids on the Algonquin and Montagnais tribes.

Long before they met the French, the Iroquois had begun to acquire French trade goods through warfare with the Indians of the St. Lawrence River. Metal goods, such as axes, were particularly desirable to the Iroquois. Like their neighbors, they had only tools they made themselves from stone, bone, and shells. It was largely the Mohawk, the easternmost of the Iroquois nations, who participated in these raiding expeditions along the St. Lawrence.

By 1609, these raids were disrupting the French and Indian fur trade in the St. Lawrence area. Samuel de Champlain, the

In the 1530s, French explorer Jacques Cartier became the first European to encounter the Iroquois when he ventured down the St. Lawrence River. At the time, there were at least eleven villages with Iroquoian-speaking people between present-day Quebec and Montreal. However, by the early 1600s, the Iroquois had been pushed out of the area and replaced by Montagnais and Algonquin people.

governor of New France and founder of the settlement of Quebec, decided to help his Indian trading partners in a campaign against the Mohawks. With a few Frenchmen and sixty warriors from the Algonquin, Montagnais, and Huron Nations, Champlain headed south down the Richelieu River and over the lake that now bears his name. At the southern end of Lake Champlain, on the evening of July 29, they encountered a party of two hundred Iroquois warriors in canoes. The Iroquois landed and immediately began to fortify their position, while their French and Indian opponents remained close together on the lake in their canoes.

It was Indian custom not to fight at night. The Iroquois said that the sun liked to see their courage. Both sides therefore spent the night preparing for the next day's battle, shouting insults at each other and boasting of their own bravery. Champlain and his two French companions kept hidden in the Montagnais' canoes during the night.

At daybreak, the Montagnais, Algonquin, and Huron warriors landed and rushed at the Iroquois, who were gathered by their fort. Suddenly, the attackers' formation divided and Champlain moved to the front. He wore a suit of half armor and an open-faced metal helmet and carried a *matchlock*-style musket. The Iroquois, who wore slatted wooden body armor for protection in battle, hesitated and stared in astonishment at this bearded creature in shiny clothing coming toward them. Before the Iroquois could recover from their surprise and let loose a hail of arrows, Champlain fired his musket at the three war chiefs whom his allies had pointed out to him. Two Mohawk chiefs were killed instantly and a third lay mortally wounded. Another Frenchman, concealed behind a tree, also fired into the group of Mohawks.

This first encounter with European firearms caused havoc among the Iroquois, and the Montagnais and their allies soon had them on the run. The attackers killed about fifty of the fleeing Iroquois and took twelve prisoners. It was a victory that firmly sealed the friendship of the French and the Indian tribes of Canada and began decades of alternating deadly conflict and diplomatic peace between the Iroquois and the French.

Another encounter between the two sides, the Battle of the Richelieu, on June 19, 1610, was even more significant than the previous year's Battle of Lake Champlain. Huron and Algonquin hunters, coming to trade their beaver pelts with the French, detected one hundred Mohawk warriors building a wooden fort along the Richelieu River. Montagnais traders, who had set up a temporary camp at the mouth of the river where it enters the St. Lawrence River, heard of this discovery. They sent to the French for military assistance to help punish the Mohawks. Champlain complied and departed with the Montagnais and a small party of Frenchmen.

At first, the battle went badly for the attackers. The Mohawk warriors repulsed a charge on their fort, killing a number of war chiefs in the process. They had devised a strategy of avoiding the French musket fire by dropping to the ground while the bullets sailed harmlessly overhead. Champlain, accustomed to the siege-warfare tactics practiced in Europe, now instructed his Indian comrades to use their shields for protection and move forward to attach ropes to the supporting logs of the fort while the French covered them with musket fire. When they pulled on the ropes, the logs toppled and the walls of the fort collapsed. When the breach in the walls was successfully made, the attackers rushed forward, killing more than eighty Mohawks and taking the remainder prisoner.

The Indian and French victory would mean an end to Iroquois raids in the St. Lawrence Valley for many years. Events to the south and east would occupy the Iroquois in the very near future.

At about the same time, the Dutch began exploring and settling along the Hudson River, and a new avenue of trade opened to the Indians of that region. Fort Orange and the upper Hudson River, site of present-day Albany, was the center of the Dutch-Indian fur trade. Unfortunately for the Mohawks, the Mahicans lived between them and the Hudson River and so were the first to benefit from the Dutch presence.

Both the Mahican and Mohawk Nations were determined to monopolize trade with the Dutch, which led to the reopening of the old Mohawk-Mahican war.

The Mohawks also attacked the Abenaki Nation in Maine and the Algonquian-speaking tribes of southern New England. The Mohawks thus opened up a new line of trade for themselves with the English settlers in this region.

In 1626, in the early phases of the Mohawk-Mahican War, the Mohawks defeated a Dutch-Mahican war party that had invaded their territory. When a Dutch trader from Fort Orange went to the Mohawks to renew friendship with them, they scolded him and the Dutch for attacking them without provocation. This incident persuaded the Dutch to seek a peaceful accommodation with the Mohawks. The Dutch would for many years put continued pressure on the Mohawk and Mahican Nations to make peace, for the constant warfare was disrupting the normal trade relations of the Dutch and the Indians.

Europeans could make great fortunes in the Indian fur trade. A continuous supply of beaver skins had become as important to the economy of the Dutch, English, and French colonies as European trade goods had become to the Indians. The items most favored by the Indians were cloth; metal goods such as knives, hoes, kettles, and axes; and firearms and ammunition. Not only were they desirable, but they were becoming essential to the Indians, who were growing increasingly dependent upon their European trade partners.

The Mohawks continued to acquire European firearms from both the Dutch and English, despite an official Dutch prohibition against trading arms with them. This made the Mohawk Nation a formidable opponent against Indian enemies and against the French in Canada. The unity of the five tribes also strengthened the Iroquois in their dealings with the outside world. Their fortunate geographical location, along the great river systems and lakes, gave them a strategic military advantage. They could travel easily and quickly over the vast inland waterways they controlled, and they could intercept enemies, attack French and Indian villages, raid the fur-laden canoes of Huron and Algonquin fur traders on their way to barter with the French, and monopolize the fur trade with the Dutch and English along the Hudson River.

As economic motivation now became a strong factor in Indian warfare, the Iroquois were in a particularly fortunate position both militarily and diplomatically. They could make alliances with competing European colonial governments whenever it seemed to their advantage. Both the Dutch and the English sought and obtained Iroquois friendship and alliances.

The French, because of their alliances with the Huron and the Algonquian-speaking Indians of Canada, were unable, despite occasional but earnest efforts, to achieve a permanent peace with the Iroquois Confederacy. The best the French could do was to protect the Iroquois religious converts their mission-aries had made during brief periods of peace by moving them to Catholic Iroquois villages they had established in Canada.

The Iroquois quickly learned to adapt their military tactics to the changing conditions of warfare. The wooden body armor that had been ample protection against stone weapons was ineffective against European firearms and the metal arrowheads acquired from the Europeans. They there-fore abandoned their useless armor and changed their style of attack. Instead of the massed charges of armored warriors on the battlefield, which had been their favored practice, they adopted a more individualistic style of warfare in which warriors fired while concealed behind trees and rocks. Stealth, surprise, and ambush were the tactics at which the Iroquois became masters. They did continue, however, to use mass surprise attacks against enemy Indian villages, where they would terrorize and overwhelm their opponents by the sheer force of their numbers and the fury of their onslaught. A steady supply of firearms obtained in trade from the English and Dutch and the joint cooperation on the warpath of two or more of the Five Nations gave the Iroquois a strong advantage over their opponents.

Economic motives were not the sole reason for an increase in Indian warfare after the arrival of the Europeans. The newcomers had brought with them diseases against which the Native Americans had no immunity and for which their healers knew no cures. Smallpox, measles, influenza, the common cold, lung infections, colic (abdominal cramps), and severe fevers were particularly deadly. Epidemics swept through Indian villages, drastically reducing their populations. The Iroquois were hit by a number of these devastating epidemics throughout the seventeenth century. For purposes of self-preservation, warfare to obtain captives for adoption became increasingly necessary for the people of the Five Nations.

In the 1630s and 1640s, the Mohawks made efforts to conclude peace agreements with various opponents in order to wage war more successfully against others. By 1643, they had settled their previous differences with the Dutch and negotiated an important treaty with them. This alliance would be permanent and would prove mutually beneficial both economically and militarily. The Dutch gained strong allies, made even stronger by their increasing supply of Dutch firearms. The Mohawks achieved more control over the fur trade, because commerce between the Dutch and the western tribes had to pass through their territory. Dutch friendship with the Mohawks also expanded to include the Iroquois tribes who lived to their west. When the English later conquered the colony of New Netherland and renamed it New York, they inherited and continued the Dutch alliance with the Iroquois.

After the Mohawks had secured Dutch friendship, they turned northward. They concluded a major peace treaty in 1645 with the French and their Huron and Algonquin allies. For the Mohawks, the peace was an opportunity to exchange prisoners and to hunt freely in the north country. The peace was also profitable for the French colonists, for it permitted the fur trade to flourish, uninterrupted by Mohawk attacks.

This tranquil situation lasted for nearly two years. When there seemed to be no more prisoners to exchange, and when peaceful hunting did not supply the Mohawks with enough furs for their insatiable trading needs, warfare broke out again. The Mohawks once more began raiding in Canada and encouraged the western tribes of the Iroquois Confederacy to attack the French and Huron.

The Iroquois were on the verge of a new era of militancy that would take them to the peak of their power on the continent. The resulting conflict marked the start of one of the most bloody and devastating series of wars in American Indian history.

5

The Expansion of Iroquois Power

The short-lived peace made by the Mohawks with the French and their Indian allies did not include the other nations of the Iroquois Confederacy. The Seneca Nation in particular continued its raids against the Wendot, or Huron, as the Europeans called them. For the Oneida, Onondaga, Cayuga, and Seneca Nations, as with the Mohawk, warfare was increasingly motivated by economic considerations. The Hurons had access to a large beaver-hunting territory and also received in trade huge supplies of beaver pelts from hunting tribes living north and west of them. The Hurons' great success in the fur trade and their access to European trade goods made them the envy of the confederacy Iroquois. Warfare in the traditional style for prestige and revenge continued, but the economic motive now gave the wars an intensity they had previously lacked. Raids for plunder became of growing importance to the Iroquois tribes in the early 1640s. They began to devastate the

Huron homeland, destroy villages, kill or take prisoner large numbers of Hurons, and carry away great quantities of furs.

An army of more than a thousand Seneca, Cayuga, and Onondaga warriors prepared to march against the Hurons in early 1647. Through vigorous peace efforts, the Hurons convinced the three central tribes of the Iroquois Confederacy—the Oneida, Onondaga, and Cayuga—that a truce would be more profitable. These Iroquois and the Hurons exchanged prisoners and valuable gifts of wampum and enjoyed several months of peace. The Mohawks and Senecas, however, kept up the pressure of their raids against the Hurons. (For additional information on this political alliance, enter "Iroquois Confederacy" into any search engine and browse the many sites listed.)

In 1648, the Dutch in the New Netherland colony adopted an official government policy of selling guns directly to the Mohawks. Governor Peter Stuyvesant fully realized that the Mohawks' demand for firearms to improve their ability to hunt was only a pretext to secure guns to wage war more effectively. Nonetheless, he approved the sale of four hundred guns directly to these Mohawk friends. Any Mohawk attack on the French or their Indian allies would benefit the Dutch, who were rivals of the French in the fur trade.

Both failure and success in war came to the Iroquois in 1648. A large Mohawk war party that had attacked a Huron fur fleet near Montreal suffered a decisive defeat, but a Seneca penetration into the Huron homeland was mostly successful.

The large Seneca army attacked the fortified Huron village of Teanaostaiaé very early on the morning of July 3, 1648. The Jesuits had established a mission in the community of about two thousand inhabitants. The Hurons were just leaving sunrise mass when the Senecas burst into town, setting fire to the longhouses, killing, and looting. The Hurons put up a spirited resistance that nearly succeeded, while their priest, Father Antoine Daniel, encouraged them and went through the

Peter Stuyvesant, who served as governor of New Netherland from 1646 to 1664, supplied guns to the Mohawks in hopes that they would attack the French and their Indian allies who were rivals of the Dutch in the fur trade.

village sprinkling the defenders, the sick, and the aged with holy water. When the tide of the battle started to turn against them, some Hurons began to flee; others gathered in the church seeking divine protection. Father Daniel urged them to flee also, and he strode out of the church to confront the enemy alone. The startled Senecas stared at him for a moment, then fired a volley of bullets and arrows at the courageous priest. They hacked his lifeless body to pieces, in accordance with their custom of showing contempt for enemies, and threw it back into the church, which had caught fire from the nearby burning longhouses. This brave confrontation by Father Daniel diverted the attention of the attackers long enough for most of the Hurons to escape.

The defeat was a serious blow to the Hurons. Seven hundred of them were either killed or taken prisoner and more than one thousand were dispersed as refugees to other Huron villages. Teanaostaiaé was permanently abandoned. It was far too late in the season for the refugees to clear new fields and plant crops. The strain on the food resources of the villages that took in these unfortunates was thus enormous. The Hurons feared that the Iroquois would attack their other villages and destroy them as well. Huron morale was low.

Shortly after their victory over the Hurons, the Senecas entered into an alliance with the Mohawks for a joint campaign into Huron country. In the fall of 1648, an army of more than a thousand Senecas and Mohawks left for the forested area north of Lake Ontario, where they lived and hunted undetected all winter. Their plan was to put themselves in an advantageous position from which to launch an attack on the Hurons when they least expected it. With the Iroquois were a number of Hurons who had been captured and adopted by the Senecas and Mohawks some years earlier. These adopted Huron war captives had become so completely integrated into Iroquois society that they now fought as loyal Iroquois warriors against their own people.

On the night of March 16, 1649, the Iroquois army silently approached the Huron village of Taenhatentaron and carefully assessed the situation. Though the village was stoutly stockaded and surrounded on three sides by ravines, it contained a number of weaknesses. Most of the inhabitants seemed to have departed several months earlier; only about four hundred were still there. Furthermore, apparently because the winter was barely over, the inhabitants felt safe from attack and carelessly had not posted sentinels on the stockade watchtowers. The advantage lay with the Iroquois. They broke with their tradition of fighting only during the daytime and took advantage of the darkness to carry out a surprise attack.

Quickly and quietly, the warriors cut through the stockade and poured into the village. In a one-sided battle the invaders soon captured the town, losing only ten men in the action. They made a rich haul of booty and captives and turned the town into a fortified Iroquois outpost. Only three Huron men escaped to raise the alarm in the countryside.

Before the night was over, a detachment of Iroquois warriors proceeded toward the mission village of St. Louis. Warned by the Hurons who had escaped from Taenhatentaron, St. Louis had braced for the coming attack. The women and children had fled toward the larger mission village of Sainte-Marie, leaving behind eighty able-bodied warriors as well as those who were too sick or feeble to make the journey. The Huron defenders of St. Louis resisted fiercely, killing thirty of the enemy before being overcome. Only two warriors escaped to carry the warning to Sainte-Marie. The Iroquois killed the sick and elderly and set fire to the village. They took their captives, including two Jesuit priests, Father Jean de Brébeuf and Gabriel Lalemant, back to Taenhatentaron for torture.

News of the calamity spread rapidly from one Huron village to another. Warriors from distant Huron settlements flocked to Sainte-Marie to defend the village against the expected Iroquois onslaught. They did not have many hours to wait.

On March 17, the greater part of the Iroquois army moved toward Sainte-Marie. The Hurons, who were scouting the countryside in anticipation of the attack, encountered about two hundred warriors, the vanguard of the invading army. After a fierce seesaw battle, the Hurons finally drove the Iroquois back to St. Louis and recaptured the village.

When the main Iroquois army caught up with the Huron victors at St. Louis, they concentrated on the reconquest of the battered village instead of continuing their march to Sainte-Marie. The battle raged well into the night, with large loss of life on both sides. By the time the Iroquois had triumphed, there were only about twenty Huron defenders left, many of whom were already wounded.

The Iroquois invaders were disheartened by the large number of casualties they suffered and the heroic stand of the Hurons. Many began to withdraw and return homeward. The Iroquois leaders decided that the best policy would be to retreat, taking with them the captives on whom they had piled great amounts of booty.

Despite the fact that the Hurons had turned back the Iroquois invasion, panic now began to seize them. They had suffered through many years of incessant raids and two years of full-scale invasions. The previous year, 1648, Iroquois raids had disrupted their farming and had caused famine conditions in some villages. Fearing that this latest Iroquois invasion was just the prelude to a long, terrifying season of warfare, the Hurons began to flee. Gathering their valuables and what little food they had and burning their villages behind them, they deserted their country and took refuge with neighboring tribes.

Some went westward to the Tionontatehronon, or Mountain People, known to the Europeans as the Petun, or Tobacco Nation. Others went southward to the Ontario Peninsula to dwell with the Neutrals, or south of Lake Erie to the Erie Nation. All of these were Iroquois people but were not members of the Iroquois Confederacy. Other Huron refugees went to Gahoendoe, or Christian Island in Canada, where there was a

Jesuit mission. Nearly eight thousand took refuge on this small island in Georgian Bay, where they suffered famine and disease and died by the thousands. By the next year, only five hundred remained alive at Gahoendoe, and these survivors left to seek refuge with the French in Quebec.

The Iroquois had achieved their main purpose. The power of the Huron Nation was forever broken.

As long as there were still nations willing to show friendship to the refugee Hurons, however, the Iroquois felt that their borders were not safe. Also, the Iroquois wanted access to these nations' valuable hunting grounds. Accordingly, they wasted little time in attacking both the Tionontatehronons and the Neutrals.

In December 1649, an Iroquois war party entered Tionontatehronon territory. Warned of their coming by the Jesuits, warriors from the village of Etharita set out to meet them. Unfortunately for them, they missed the Iroquois, who had taken another route. Frustrated in their search, the warriors of Etharita returned to their village only to find it in ashes. Stunned by their failure to stop the enemy and by the severity of their loss, the warriors sat silently for half a day in mourning and shame.

By the spring of 1650, the surviving members of the Tionontatehronon Nation, along with their Huron companions, left their homeland and dispersed westward. This merged group, later known as Wyandot, wandered for years seeking a permanent home. By the mid-eighteenth century, most Wyandots had settled in two areas: on the banks of the Detroit River and along the Sandusky River in Ohio country. Land pressures from non-Indian settlers later forced them to move, and in the nineteenth century, they journeyed west, first to Kansas and then to Indian Territory (later to become the state of Oklahoma). Here, a refugee group of Senecas offered them land along the Neosho River. Adversity would at last make friends of these former enemies.

In 1651, an army of Senecas invaded Neutral country. They were victorious at first, but the Neutrals finally defeated them and drove them back. The Iroquois returned a few months later, this time destroying the main Neutral town. They left with much booty and many captives. Now the hard-pressed Neutrals also abandoned their territory to the Iroquois and moved west to the vicinity of Saginaw Bay. From there, they may eventually have moved south to the Ohio Valley. Wherever they went, these Neutrals were henceforth lost to history.

After the total defeat of these Indian allies of the French, the four western nations of the Iroquois Confederacy sought to replace them as trading partners of the French. Irritated and greatly inconvenienced by Mohawk control over trade with the Dutch, these tribes were eager for a new source of commerce. The Seneca, Cayuga, Onondaga, and Oneida Nations therefore made peaceful overtures in 1653 to the French along the St. Lawrence. The French gladly assented, much relieved to be at peace with these troublesome Iroquois. The stable period that followed permitted a French Catholic mission and a trading post to be established at Onondaga.

Alarmed at being bypassed by their western associates, the Mohawks also concluded a peace with the French. During the next few months, however, they saw the Onondagas prospering and growing in both power and prestige as a result of their French alliance.

In a conference with the French at Quebec in 1654, the Mohawks made known their displeasure with the French attentions to the Onondagas. Their spokesman was a mixed-blood chief named Canaqueese, known to the Dutch as Jan Smits, son of a Dutch father and a Mohawk mother. Canaqueese described the political structure of the Extended Lodge to the French, informing them that the Mohawks were the Keepers of the Eastern Door and represented the proper entry to the confederacy. He berated the French for wrongfully entering the Lodge through the smoke hole (Onondaga), like a thief, rather than correctly through the front door. Despite this rebuke, the French continued to favor the Onondagas as trading partners.

Nothing could better illustrate the continuing tensions and rivalries that existed within the League itself than this speech by Canaqueese. Although the Five Nations were technically united, they were not always of the same mind.

The western Iroquois next turned their attention to the Erie Nation, who lived west of the Seneca Nation and south of Lake Erie. They were also an Iroquoian people but were never members of the League. Their presence in the Ohio Valley kept the Senecas from using that region as a hunting territory. Because the Eries also harbored Huron and Neutral refugees among them, the Senecas felt that their borders were unsafe. Furthermore, the Eries had angered the Onondagas by attacking and defeating an Onondaga war party in southern Ontario. Growing anti-Erie sentiment among the Iroquois soon resulted in a three-year war. By 1657, the Eries were totally defeated and dispersed; many were adopted by the Onondagas and Senecas. The remainder fled, maintaining their ethnic identity for a while but later disappearing as a separate identifiable group.

Within a decade, the Iroquois had completely smashed the great trading nations to the north and west of them, emerging as rulers over a vast domain. They had incorporated through adoption several thousand of their former rivals and thus considerably strengthened their confederacy. Had they been contented with their victories up to this point, and with exploiting the resources of the country they had just won, they might have enjoyed the rest of the century in peace. Instead they engaged in nearly forty years of ruinous warfare from which, despite initial successes, they finally emerged in a much weakened state.

The Susquehannock, a powerful Iroquoian tribe living south of the Iroquois Confederacy in Maryland and Pennsylvania, had a far-flung trading network, both with other Indian nations and with the nearby European colonists in Maryland, Delaware, and Virginia. They had been engaged in blood feuds with the confederacy Iroquois for well over a century. Flushed with their victory over the Hurons and their allies, the Iroquois, especially the Senecas and Mohawks, now turned against the Susquehannocks. They found these southerners no easy mark, for they were skilled warriors, living in stoutly fortified towns and well armed with European weapons, including cannons. It took twenty years of debilitating warfare for the Iroquois to conquer them.

Meanwhile, the peace that the French and Iroquois had made in 1653 was beginning to crumble. The Mohawks, jealous of the Onondagas' growing importance as a result of their French alliance, made plans to destroy the French mission at Onondaga. There was also resentment against the Jesuits among residents of Onondaga because of the diseases the French had inadvertently brought with them and to which the Indians had no immunity. Moreover, the new Christian religion of the Jesuits had begun to fragment the community. Followers of the Jesuits were no longer participating in the traditional ceremonies. This led some of the traditionalist Onondagas to plan an attack against the missionaries. Warned of the approaching danger by Iroquois friends, the Jesuits fled.

The Mohawks resumed hostilities along the Ottawa and St. Lawrence Rivers in Canada, and Iroquois warriors attacked Indian allies of the French in the upper Great Lakes region. The French were rapidly becoming exasperated with the Iroquois.

In 1664, the English conquered New Netherland and renamed it New York. These newcomers lost little time in negotiating treaties of friendship with the Indian allies of the Dutch. Fort Orange was renamed Albany and became the center of English treaty-making with the Iroquois. The

English alliance with the Five Nations would be of great significance to both sides during the various power struggles on the North American continent over the next hundred years. The Iroquois, with their favorable geographic location along the lakes and rivers of central and western New York, commanded the entire transportation network through their region as well as major routes to the west and south. They were thus in a strategically strong position both commercially and militarily.

Also in 1664, the French made a firm decision to block continued Iroquois aggressions against them and their allies. King Louis XIV of France sent the renowned Carnigan-Salières regiment to his American colony. These troops were under the command of the able veteran officer, the Marquis Prouville de Tracy. The king's instructions to the governor of New France were to initiate a military expedition against the Iroquois to "carry war even to their friends in order . . . to exterminate them."

News of the arrival of the French regiment spread rapidly throughout the country of the Extended Lodge. Representatives of the four western nations of the Iroquois Confederacy hastened to Canada to make peace with the French. The Mohawks stubbornly held out, complaining that the French had sent no official notice to them. Tracy, determined that his troops would be the official messengers to the recalcitrant Mohawks, launched an invasion of their territory in January 1666. Thwarted by the bitter winter weather and a Mohawk ambush, the French soon returned to Canada. They had, however, made their point, and the Mohawks asked to be included in the peace.

Tracy soon claimed that the Mohawks were not abiding by the terms of the peace and so launched another invasion against them in the fall of 1666. This time, he was successful. The French troops burned a hastily abandoned Mohawk village and destroyed all the crops and stored food supplies.

Obviously, the French did not intend to melt away before the Iroquois as the Hurons, the Neutrals, and others had done.

From then on, when peace treaties failed to secure the desired results, the French would resort to destructive military invasions of Iroquois country. The Five Nations now had a determined and formidable foe to face—a foe that would no longer remain quiet while the Five Nations attacked its Indian allies and undermined France's economic and political interests on the North American continent.

6

Warfare and Diplomacy

During their brief interlude of peace with the Iroquois, the French missionaries had been remarkably successful in making converts. In 1667 and 1668, a small group of Oneidas established themselves along the St. Lawrence River, near the French settlement of Montreal. These Oneidas became the nucleus of a rapidly growing village of Catholic Iroquois. Onondagas, Hurons, and especially Mohawks swelled the population of the village, which took the name *Caughnawaga* (At the Rapids).

The Caughnawaga became firm allies of the French, even joining with them in military expeditions against the Iroquois in their old homeland south of Lake Ontario. Throughout the century of conflict between the French and English for predominance in North America, the Caughnawaga continued to support the French.

The Iroquois attacks on the tribes of the western Great Lakes region in the late seventeenth century gradually merged with the

European wars between the French and the English that had spilled over to the North American continent. The French intervention against the Iroquois in support of their own Indian allies would prove to be a serious obstacle to Iroquois ambitions.

The Iroquois did gain, at least in the short run, from their alliance with the English. When Edmund Andros became governor of the colony of New York in 1674, he proceeded immediately to renew and strengthen English alliances with all the Algonquian and Iroquois groups within New York's borders. In the earliest Dutch period, the Indians and Dutch had used the metaphor of "chains" to describe their alliances: "We are brothers and are joined together by chains." The implication was that nothing could break this "Covenant Chain" and disrupt the friendship. Governor Andros expanded this Covenant Chain tradition to attach the Iroquois more firmly to the English and to promote the interests of his New York colony. He forbade other English colonies to make any treaties with New York's Indian tribes unless sponsored by the New York government. In 1667, he permitted delegates from Maryland and Virginia to come to Albany, New York, to conduct peace negotiations with the Five Nations, whose warriors had recently been attacking the Indian tribes in those two colonies to the south. As a result of these negotiations, the Five Nations took Maryland and Virginia into the Covenant Chain. This enhanced the prestige and power of the colony of New York, securing English friendship for the Iroquois. It also enhanced the power of the Iroquois Confederacy by enabling them to incorporate other formerly hostile Indian tribes into the Extended Lodge.

The Covenant Chain would be manipulated by both the Five Nations and the English to increase their advantage over their opponents. The English now had the friendship of the most powerful Indian confederacy on the continent. The Iroquois, for their part, had made a valuable military and economic alliance with the aggressive English and had secured their borders to the east and south. To the north and west, however, were the French and their Indian allies and trading partners. In these regions, the Iroquois could feel no security except through warfare and conquest.

Beginning in 1680, the Iroquois carried on a devastating series of wars against these western Indians. The fur trade had become as important to the Iroquois as it was to the Europeans, and they determined to open new areas of supply. In one campaign after another, they attacked the Illinois and Miami Indians of the Ohio and Illinois region, destroying their villages and killing or capturing huge numbers from each tribe. They alternately threatened and cajoled the Ottawa Indians north of the Great Lakes, who supplied the French with two-thirds of their furs. The French had a string of forts in the Illinois and upper Great Lakes regions. Seeing their position dangerously threatened by repeated Iroquois aggressions, they decided to intervene.

In June 1687, Jacques-René de Brisay Denonville, the governor of New France, led an invading force of more than two thousand French and Indians against the Senecas, destroying their villages, their standing crops, and their stored grain. The next year, the Cayuga, Onondaga, and Oneida Nations traveled to Montreal to negotiate a treaty with Denonville. The peace would not last long. Less than two years later, King William's War (1689–1697) broke out between France and England. The Iroquois seized the opportunity and once more went on the offensive against the French, attacking the settlement of Lachine, not far from Montreal.

The French continually retaliated against the English and their Iroquois allies during the course of the war. In February 1690, the new governor of New France, Louis de Buade de Frontenac, with a force of 210 French troops and Caughnawaga Indian allies, attacked and destroyed the English village of Schenectady, northwest of Albany. Three years later, in 1693, Frontenac surprised and destroyed the three Mohawk villages and took three hundred captives. In July 1696, with 2,200

French and Indian troops, he successfully attacked the Oneidas and again the Onondagas.

In the western Great Lakes region, the Ojibwas led a coalition of Ottawas and Potawatomis known as the Council of the Three Fires. The warriors of the Three Fires hammered the Iroquois relentlessly and in three fierce battles in 1696 drove them out of the Ontario Peninsula and claimed it as their own.

The Iroquois suffered an enormous number of casualties in these western wars. Instead of achieving their purpose, they who had once been the invincible conquerors of a vast territory were now themselves defeated. In the last decade of the seventeenth century alone, they had lost at least sixteen hundred and perhaps as many as two thousand of their own people. They had seen their homeland invaded and destroyed again and again by the French and their Indian allies. Now their western landholdings were being destroyed as well.

The Iroquois decided that the time had come for a new strategy. In early 1700, they sent out peace feelers to Governor Louis-Hector de Callière of New France. The governor responded favorably but insisted that the Indian allies of the French also be included in the peace. Both sides promised to return their prisoners and the Iroquois further requested the resumption of trade with the French and access to their smiths, who could repair their guns and tools. They reminded the governor that they were making peace with him despite English disapproval and so asked for his protection should the English try to punish them. Governor Callière gladly agreed to all of the Iroquois requests. Both sides set August 1701 as the date for a great gathering at Montreal when the final treaty would be approved by all the warring parties.

The chief author of this new peace policy was the Onondaga statesman *Teganissorens*, pronounced by the English as *Decanesora*. He was the greatest orator of his day. One New Yorker who was acquainted with him likened him to the great ancient Roman statesman Cicero. A man of abundant wisdom and ability and a

true patriot, Teganissorens realized that the Iroquois' best interests lay in maintaining neutrality between the French and the
English, not letting either European nation gain a predominance
of power. The most important task for the Iroquois was now to
preserve their own territory and their independence.

The new peace policy brought social and economic benefits
to the Iroquois. Freed from danger from the north and west,
they could now hunt and even settle in the Ohio region without fear of attack. They had granted the western Great Lakes
Indians the right to travel through their territory to trade with
them and with the English. The Iroquois profited greatly from
this commerce, because they received additional furs from
these western Indians in exchange for the goods and food they
supplied to the journeyers. The Iroquois could also trade with
the French at Fort Frontenac on the northeastern shore of Lake
Ontario, as well as at the new small trading post opened by the
French at Irondequoit on the south shore of Lake Ontario.

When the French established a trading post at Niagara and
a few years later strengthened it by building a large stone fort,
the Iroquois became alarmed at such a formidable military
presence in their territory. They therefore permitted the British
to build a fort at the mouth of the Oswego River and Lake
Ontario. The French instantly recognized the Iroquois strategy
of balancing one European nation against another.

For most of the next half century, the Iroquois lapsed
only occasionally from their policy of neutrality. This policy
was often under great strain, however, for pro-French and
pro-English factions had developed within each tribe of the
Five Nations. The strongest French advocates were among
the Senecas and Onondagas. The English had more supporters
among the Mohawks, who lived closer to Albany and the English
settlements. During the various phases of Queen Anne's War
(1702–1713), King George's War (1744–1748), and the French
and Indian War (1754–1763), the English were always able
to rouse a number of Iroquois warriors to accompany their

expeditions against the French. Despite these violations of the peace by individual warriors, the neutrality policy continued until the middle of the eighteenth century. The long period of peace enabled the Iroquois to rebuild their communities, increase their population, and expand their trade.

The English as well as the French recognized the political importance of establishing religious missions among the Indians they wished to attach to their cause. The Jesuits had been depleting the population of Iroquois country for years by luring large numbers of converts to their Catholic village of Caughnawaga, near Montreal. In 1749, the Sulpician missionary Abbé François Picquet established a mission, La Presentation, at the point where the Oswegatchie River and the St. Lawrence River meet (present-day Ogdensburg, New York). The former village was composed mostly of Mohawks and the latter mostly of Onondagas and Cayugas and some Oneidas. Around 1750, a group of Caughnawagas settled farther up the St. Lawrence River, where the French established a mission named St. Regis. Jesuit missionaries continued to be active among the Iroquois who remained in their homeland, where a number of converts, loyal both to their new faith and to the French who had converted them and who continued to show them favor, still lived. By about 1806, under pressure from American settlers in the region, the Oswegatchie settlement was abandoned and many of its inhabitants moved to the St. Regis community and merged with the Mohawks.

The English were quick to learn the lesson and to take an interest in ministering to the Iroquois. The earliest efforts of English missionaries among the Mohawks, however, met with little response.

For many years, Dutch Reformed pastors who lived in or near Albany had also ministered to their Mahican and Mohawk neighbors and had made a number of converts. One of them was Tee Yee Neen Ha Ga Row, known by his baptismal name of Hendrick, a Mohawk of the Wolf clan living in the lower

Mohawk village of Tiononderoge, near Fort Hunter. He was converted to the Protestant faith by the Dutch pastor Godfrey Dellius. Hendrick subsequently became one of the prominent leaders among the Christian Mohawks. Dellius, however, misused his trust among the Mohawks by persuading the illiterate

A Woman To Be Venerated

Among the Mohawks who moved to Caughnawaga in 1667 was a young woman, Tekakwitha, who was living in the longhouse of her uncle. She had been born in 1656. Her mother, a Christian Algonquin, had been captured by a band of Mohawks at Three Rivers, near Quebec, and married a Mohawk chief, which saved her from death or slavery. When Tekakwitha was about four years old, her parents and younger brother died in a smallpox epidemic. She alone of her family recovered, her eyesight permanently damaged and her skin pockmarked. She was adopted and cared for by her father's brother, a village chief, and so she learned the ways of her Mohawk people.

French attacks in 1666 destroyed Tekakwitha's village. The surviving Mohawks moved farther west, joining other refugee Iroquois at Caughnawaga, near Montreal, and finally making peace with the French. Several Jesuit missionaries came to Caughnawaga in 1667 and stayed for three days in Tekakwitha's uncle's longhouse. Two years later, construction began on St. Peter's Chapel in the village. When Tekakwitha was nineteen years old, she asked the Jesuits to give her instruction in the Catholic faith. She resisted the efforts of her relatives to arrange a marriage for her in the Indian way. On Easter Sunday in 1676, she was baptized as Catherine (Katherine in English, Kateri in the Mohawk language).

Many Mohawks in the village observed traditional beliefs, and they harassed those who, like Kateri, attempted to observe the Christian faith. Stones were thrown at her when she refused to work in the cornfields on Sundays. She decided to take the earliest opportunity to leave Caughnawaga for the St. Francis mission south of the St. Lawrence River in Canada, at Sault St. Louis. Her chance came in late 1677 when three Christian Indians from St. Francis, one of them a relative of hers, came to visit Caughnawaga. Her uncle was away at the time and unable to prevent her departure.

Indians to put their marks to three deeds granting vast tracts of land to him and his politically connected friends. Hendrick and another Mohawk leader traveled to New York City to complain about the fraud before the governor, the Earl of Bellomont, and were eventually successful in seeing these fraudulent grants

Tekakwitha took her first communion at the mission before Christmas that same year. A few months later, she was accepted into the Society of the Holy Family and took a vow never to marry. Despite her physical disabilities and daily attendance at services, she continued to carry out her traditional Indian work obligations when they did not interfere with her religious observances.

Her health had been poor since childhood, and in early 1680, she became quite ill. She died a few months later, on April 17, only twenty-four years of age. The priest who attended her reported to all his wonder at seeing her pockmarked face become clear and beautiful.

Kateri Tekakwitha immediately became the subject of prayer and reverence. French as well as Indian Christians visited her grave with personal prayers, and their devotion was often rewarded. Two Jesuits published works about her before the end of the seventeenth century. In the early twentieth century, her followers were successful in getting the Vatican to take the first steps that could eventually lead to sainthood for Kateri. In 1932, she was declared venerable. An investigation was authorized into the "Cause of Catherine Tekakwitha," and documents on her behalf were gathered (published in English in 1940 by Fordham University Press in New York City). Three hundred years after her death, on June 22, 1980, she was accorded the second step leading to sainthood and was beatified. Her advocates continue to visit the National Shrine of North American Martyrs in Auriesville, New York, near the village in which Kateri was born and spent most of her life, as well as the Saint Francis Xavier Mission in Caughnawaga and Sault St. Louis near Montreal in Canada, where she died. Only the final step of canonization remains to make Kateri Tekakwitha the first American Indian saint.

revoked by the governor and the assembly in 1699. Governor Bellomont also suspended Dellius from his ministry.

In 1710, during Queen Anne's War, English officials at Albany were disturbed about their government's lack of interest in Indian affairs. They therefore decided to send a delegation to England to emphasize the importance of holding on to Indian support. Colonel Francis Nicholson and Peter Schuyler took with them four chiefs: Hendrick, two other Mohawks, and a Mahican. Schuyler, a former mayor of Albany and a wealthy fur trader, had many years' experience in negotiating with Indians on behalf of the city of Albany and the colony of New York. He was held in particularly high regard by the Iroquois, who had come to consider him their special intermediary with the colonial government.

In London, the Indians were a sensation. They were entertained everywhere, had their portraits painted, and were presented at court. The "Four Kings," as they were known in England, asked Queen Anne to send help to combat the French and to provide Church of England missionaries for the Indian villages. The queen assented and became the patron of the Mohawk mission.

The Anglican missionary organization, the Society for Propagating the Gospel, had increased success in the years that followed in converting the Mohawks to the Anglican faith. The missionaries also devised a system of writing the Mohawk language, provided schooling for young Mohawks, and translated religious literature into Mohawk. By the 1740s, most Mohawks were at least nominal Protestant Christians and were firm friends of the English.

So loyal were the Mohawks that in later years, the English would often refer to them as "the faithful Mohawks." One of the most faithful was Hendrick Peters, or Theyanoguin, a member of the Bear clan from the upper Mohawk village of Canajoharie. Because of his chiefly status, the English often called him King Hendrick. In 1755, when he was well past sixty years of age, he

Sa Ga Yeath Qua Pieth Tow of the Mohawk Bear clan visited England in 1710. He was known to the English as Brant and may have been the grandfather of Joseph Brant.

would put himself at the head of three hundred warriors and join the English in an expedition against the French. At a battle near Lake George in the Adirondacks, the English and Mohawks would defeat the invading French Army, but the courageous Hendrick would lose his life.

But in the early eighteenth century, as a result of the peace settlement of 1701 following their defeats in the 1690s, the Iroquois sought ways to regain power. Military means were closed to them, so they turned to political efforts. A part of their strategy was to cooperate with the government of Pennsylvania and to assert the authority of the Iroquois Confederacy over the Indian tribes of that region. These Pennsylvania tribes were the Lenni-Lenape (Delaware), Shawnee, Conestoga (the remnant of the Susquehannock), and Conoy (Piscataway). Pennsylvania officials saw an advantage in developing a special friendship with the Iroquois, because the confederacy could help control the tribes within their borders. They were particularly concerned that the Shawnees had become too friendly with the French. This "Pennsylvania policy" was thus mutually beneficial to Pennsylvania and the Iroquois.

After the Iroquois had agreed not to fight against France's Indian allies in the west, they turned their hostilities against the Indians of the south. In a long series of wars lasting more than fifty years, mainly against the Catawba and the Cherokee tribes in the Carolinas and Georgia, the Iroquois gained both prestige and captives. The English repeatedly tried to get the Iroquois to stop these attacks on their Indian allies, but the League persisted. They had everything to gain and nothing to lose. The French and their western Indian allies benefited by these wars, for the French had colonial interests in the south and were delighted to see English allies being destroyed. Once more, the Iroquois were emerging as a force to be reckoned with.

The Iroquois' wars in the south brought them in touch with the problems of the Tuscarora tribe in North Carolina. The Tuscarora was an Iroquois group that had migrated south before the formation of the confederacy but who still remembered their kinship with the northern tribes. Their non-Indian neighbors in North Carolina had for many years been encroaching upon their lands and kidnapping their children to sell into slavery. Pressed beyond their endurance, the Tuscaroras declared war on the colonists. The North Carolinians received the military support of colonists and various Indian allies, including the Catawbas, the Cherokees, and the Yamasees, from South Carolina. The Tuscaroras, defeated in the 1711–1713 wars, migrated north to Pennsylvania and New York to take refuge in the Extended Lodge. The Oneidas adopted them and they became the sixth tribe of the League. The Five Nations, now strengthened and enlarged, would from this time on be known as the Six Nations.

The Iroquois were able to play their neutrality game between the French and English only until the end of the French and Indian War (1754–1763). After that, the victorious English deprived France of its American colonies and emerged as the major power on the East Coast, in Canada, and in the Ohio region. Even during that war, the Iroquois had not been completely neutral, nor were they united in taking sides. The Mohawks had generally supported the English and the Senecas had fought with the pro-French Indians. Now the English occupied former French forts in Canada and the West, and they were far less accommodating to the Indians than the French had been. They had no need to be overly generous to the Indians, who could no longer ally themselves with the French.

Indian resentment against the English flared up in a brief war known as Pontiac's Conspiracy (1763–1764), after the Ottawa war leader who organized this rebellion. The Senecas took an enthusiastic part in this uprising, attempting to drive the British out of the west. The war failed in its objective and was soon over.

Sir William Johnson, the superintendent of Indian affairs for the northern department of Great Britain's American colonies, scolded the Senecas for their part in the war. As punishment, he forced them to cede some of their territory to the Crown.

Johnson had come to America from Ireland in 1738 to manage the Mohawk Valley estate of his absentee uncle,

Admiral Peter Warren. With financial help from Warren, Johnson acquired more and more land in that area, employing white servants and black slaves to work his property. He also went into business, importing goods from England to exchange for Iroquois furs. His farming and trading enterprises both prospered. He had been adopted by the Mohawks and was thoroughly acquainted with their culture. A Mohawk woman, Mary Brant (or Molly Brant, as she was better known), served as his housekeeper and his wife. Although he never legally married her, he treated her with great respect and affection. He raised all his children by her in the style becoming the sons and daughters of an English country gentleman. His wealth and community standing, combined with his good relationship with the Iroquois, led to the government appointment to manage Indian affairs, a post in which he served for years.

In the years following Pontiac's War, while Sir William Johnson was urging the Six Nations to hold fast to the Covenant Chain, trouble was brewing in the colonies. The settlers were becoming rebellious and protesting against British taxes. Johnson was concerned that the growing quarrel between the colonists and the Crown might disrupt the British-Indian alliances. He was particularly worried about the missionary to the Oneidas, Samuel Kirkland, who also worked among the Tuscaroras. Kirkland was not a member of the Church of England but was instead a New England Puritan. He sided with the colonists, not with their British government. Johnson tried to remove Kirkland but found that Oneida members of his church stood solidly behind their missionary.

Johnson died suddenly in 1774, during a treaty council with the Iroquois. He was succeeded in office by his nephew, Colonel Guy Johnson. It was now Guy Johnson's task to hold the Iroquois loyal to the Crown as the colonists headed toward separation from Great Britain.

The American Revolution had a tragic impact on the Six Nations. The neutrality they had sought to maintain between contending parties broke down under pressures from the British and the colonists. The warfare that erupted in the country surrounding the Six Nations Confederacy eventually drew them all into the conflict, and they were not all of the same mind. Two of the most active Mohawk supporters of the Crown were Molly Brant and her younger brother Joseph, an energetic war chief. Meanwhile, the Oneidas had begun to enlist in the militia units being formed in towns in the Mohawk River valley to fight against the Loyalists, colonists who sided with the British.

In previous wars, when the Iroquois nations had divergent allegiances, they had been able to fight their respective opponents without fighting one another. The American Revolution would change all that. The confederacy council could not control the warriors in each nation. Each nation therefore chose sides for itself. The Oneida and Tuscarora Nations chose the new American union. The Mohawk, Onondaga, Cayuga, and Seneca Nations chose the British king. The hostilities that raged through their own country and the surrounding non-Indian settlements meant that on more than one occasion, Iroquois was fighting Iroquois.

So destructive were the raids of the pro-British Iroquois and Loyalists that the government of New York appealed to the Continental Congress (the legislative body created by the Americans to govern the former colonies during the war) for help. In 1779, General George Washington authorized an invasion of Iroquois country. The officer in charge of the expedition was Major General John Sullivan. A companion army under Brigadier General James Clinton joined Sullivan. In the fall, the two armies set off on what was to be the successful destruction of all the hostile Indian villages east of the Genesee River.

The Sullivan-Clinton campaign pushed the Loyalist Iroquois back to Fort Niagara. Here, the British Army and Indian Department were forced to protect and provide for the starving and homeless Indians throughout the severe winter that followed.

Joseph Brant served as an officer in the British military during the American Revolution and led warriors of the Mohawk, Onondaga, Cayuga, and Seneca Nations on raids against those who opposed the Crown. After the war, Brant settled at the Grand River Reservation in Ontario, which is now known as the Six Nations Reserve. Nearby Brantford, Ontario, bears his name.

The American invasion did not defeat the Iroquois but merely increased their desire for revenge. The following spring, the Indians came back with even more ferocity. Joseph Brant, although not the leading warrior of the confederacy, became particularly active throughout the war. He led a raiding party that burned the Oneida and Tuscarora villages in retaliation for their support of the Americans.

The most distinguished warrior of the League was *Kayengkwaahton*, or "Old Smoke," of the Senecas. Now elderly but still vigorous, he usually had to ride a horse on long marches in order to keep up with the younger warriors. The young Cornplanter, another Seneca, also held one of the leading positions as war chief of the confederacy.

The British completely ignored their Indian allies when they signed the Treaty of Paris, which ended the war with the United States in 1783. The Iroquois were horrified and incensed at what they considered a betrayal of their loyal services. British officers still in North America were also embarrassed by their government's neglect of the Indians whom, after all, they had enticed into the war. General Frederick Haldimand, commander of the British forces in Canada, pressured his government to grant land to the Loyalist Iroquois so they would not be left to the revenge of the victors.

The British government gave its approval and Haldimand bought a large tract of land from the Mississauga Indians along the Grand River on the Ontario Peninsula. He presented it to the Mohawks and the other Loyalist Iroquois—"His Majesty's faithful Allies," as the general called them. Most of the Loyalist Iroquois who wished to migrate followed Joseph Brant to Grand River. Another group of Mohawks, under John Deserontyon, settled north of the Bay of Quinté, with Haldimand's help.

On the Grand River Reservation, there were members of all the Six Nations. It is known today as the Six Nations Reserve. Most Senecas, however, elected to remain in their own country rather than emigrate to Canada.

After centuries of conquest and domination, the Extended Lodge was now disrupted and its nations dispersed. The Iroquois were beginning a new phase in their history: the *reservation* period.

7

Decline and Revival

Because many pro-British Iroquois moved to the Grand River Reservation in Canada after the American Revolution, the geographic organization of the Extended Lodge was disrupted. The Mohawks were no longer actually Keepers of the Eastern Door, for they had all abandoned their former home territory along the Mohawk River. The only Mohawk group still remaining in New York was the St. Regis settlement in the far north, along the St. Lawrence River. The people here were Catholics who had earlier moved to a Jesuit community and were not members of the confederacy. Many Onondagas and Cayugas had gone westward to live among the Senecas at Buffalo Creek (site of the present-day city of Buffalo).

Despite the division and disruption of the League, the leaders on both sides of the border attempted to mend the breach and reorganize the confederacy. They moved their council fire from its ancient seat at Onondaga to Buffalo Creek, which was now their most central location. The wampum of the confederacy was also transferred to Buffalo Creek.

For a number of years, this arrangement worked and the confederacy continued to function. Iroquois from all the villages would travel to Buffalo Creek for the important confederacy council meetings and diplomatic transactions. Only later did the confederacy become divided by the United States–Canadian border.

After the end of the American Revolution and the signing of the peace treaty between the United States and Great Britain, the Continental Congress appointed commissioners to make peace with the four hostile Iroquois nations—the Mohawk, Onondaga, Cayuga, and Seneca. The commissioners traveled with a military guard to Fort Stanwix, near Oneida Lake. The Treaty of Fort Stanwix, signed on October 22, 1784, was an imposed peace, not a peace between equals. The Loyalist Iroquois claimed that they had not been defeated in battle by the United States. But now that they lacked British military support, they were unable to defend their sovereignty or their land rights. From the Indians' point of view, the British had not only deserted them but had turned their whole country over to the United States under the terms of the Treaty of Paris. Intimidated by the presence of soldiers and the aggressive behavior and demands of the U.S. commissioners, the Iroquois had no alternative but to agree to the terms being imposed on them.

The Treaty of Fort Stanwix brought peace to the four hostile tribes and assured the two faithful tribes, the Oneida and Tuscarora, of continued peaceful possession of their land. The commissioners took six delegates from the hostile tribes as hostages to assure the safe return of war prisoners still held by those tribes. The treaty set a boundary defining the limits of the Iroquois country. The new limits deprived them of much Seneca land in western New York and Pennsylvania and all the Ohio lands.

When the commissioners from the Continental Congress had concluded their treaty with the browbeaten Iroquois, commissioners from Pennsylvania stepped forward to negotiate a large land grant on behalf of their own *state*. As payment, they offered the Indians $4,000 worth of goods, telling them that the land already belonged to Pennsylvania by the terms of the peace treaty with Great Britain. Confused and demoralized, the Iroquois delegates nonetheless did manage to secure another $1,000 worth of goods from the Pennsylvania delegates before finally agreeing. On October 23, 1784, they signed away a large tract of land in northwestern Pennsylvania.

Greatly angered by the loss of land agreed to by their delegates, the Six Nations council meeting at Buffalo Creek refused to ratify the Treaty of Fort Stanwix and even offered to return the gifts given to the delegates. Their protest was fruitless. As far as the U.S. government was concerned, the treaty was valid, whether the whole confederated Six Nations in council approved or not. The tactic of conquest by treaty would be used continually in the future in United States–Indian relations.

Those Iroquois who had gone to Canada had other difficulties. The tract of land along the Grand River was large but not as vast as the territory the Mohawks and their friends had left behind in their own country. Joseph Brant, or Thayendanegea, who emerged as the outstanding leader of the Six Nations Reserve, as their homeland in Canada was called, saw that there was too little land to support a hunting economy but more than could be farmed by the women in the present population. Most of the Indian men refused to take up farming because it was traditionally the women's occupation. Brant saw that with hunting now restricted because of the smaller land base, farmers would have to raise substantial herds of domestic animals to provide meat. In order to put greater acreage into production than could be done with hand tools, the Indians would also have to use horse-drawn plows and harrows in breaking up and cultivating the ground. The effective use of these heavy implements called for greater physical strength than most women had.

Brant devised a plan to help his people make the transition to reservation living. He firmly believed that it would be necessary for the men to change their attitudes and adopt the non-Indians' style of farming to provide enough food for the whole population. To encourage the Indian men to become farmers, Brant proposed and other Iroquois leaders agreed to lease or sell parcels of their reservation to friendly non-Indian farmers. Brant had the support of the leading chief at Grand River, Henry Tekarihoga, *sachem* of the Turtle clan, who was Brant's wife's brother. Numbers of nearby whites, many of whom had fought beside the Indians in the recent war, gained grants on the Six Nations Reserve. And gradually, Indian men did begin to farm. Brant's program was thus successful, but only partially so, for it caused ongoing disputes.

British officials in Canada were determined that the Iroquois should not sell or lease any of their land to outsiders. It was meant for Indians only. Officials constantly warned Brant that the king's allies (the Iroquois) should not have the king's subjects (the English) as tenants. For years, Brant conducted a running feud with the government representatives, insisting that the Indians should be able to do whatever they wanted with their own land.

In the end, Brant had his way, but the results were not always what he and his supporters had wished. The property deeds were often so poorly drawn and the agreements so negligently enforced that the Six Nations Council frequently did not receive its lease money. Eventually, huge parcels of reservation land passed out of the Indians' control. More than 350,000 acres of reservation land were lost as a result of Brant's program.

His policy also led to factionalism on the Six Nations Reserve. Some people were bitterly opposed to granting any of their land to the whites. Many began to gossip that Brant was corrupt and was pocketing the lease money himself—a charge that was completely untrue.

The ultimate failure of the land-grant policy to provide the tribe with income and the great loss of reservation territory were not the result of corruption on the part of any member of the Six Nations Council. These problems stemmed from the Indians' lack of knowledge of the complexities of English real estate law and lack of experience as landlords and real estate entrepreneurs. To be successful in any enterprise involving land as a commodity and whites as purchasers or tenants, they would have had to know a great deal—how to survey lands, write deeds, keep records, collect rents and mortgage payments, and wisely invest the money received. They would also have had to know how to bring lawsuits against those who were delinquent in payments, hire competent and honest lawyers, carry out foreclosure proceedings, as well as find money to pay for lawyers and long-drawn-out legal maneuvers. Real estate was a business in which the Iroquois were at a decided disadvantage. Even the non-Indian trustees later chosen to handle the Six Nations' finances made serious blunders and invested the Six Nations' income in a canal-building enterprise that failed dismally.

Long after Brant's death, non-Indians continued to be persistent trespassers on the reservation and continued to pressure the Indians to sell more land to them. In response to government concern that the reservation would soon dwindle away to nothing, the chiefs in 1841 voluntarily surrendered most of their remaining land to the British Crown. They retained a smaller reserve that could be more easily managed and that would be forever guaranteed to them. The government officials then proceeded to evict the non-Indian *squatters*—illegal settlers—from the reserve. This was not easy but was eventually successful.

The confederacy Iroquois on the American side of the border did little better than the community in Canada in preserving their lands. The 1784 Treaty of Fort Stanwix had promised the Iroquois rights to peaceful occupation of their territory, then comprising most of central and western New York. But by 1800, all that remained of that huge territory were a few small reservations. New York State officials, under the leadership of Governor George Clinton, relentlessly pressured the Iroquois to sell out. These officials planned to confine Indians to a few small villages in order to acquire the rest of their land, which they would sell to non-Indians.

First, the state officials and then agents of private land companies independently made treaties with the Iroquois tribes, successfully whittling away the Indians' domain. The directors of the land companies in particular anticipated huge profits from the sale of this vast territory to settlers. State officials wanted to populate western New York with non-Indians, who would carve out farms from the forest, build villages and cities, and thus strengthen the state politically and economically. In the process, the Iroquois lost out. The Oneida Reservation was reduced to a few acres. The Cayugas sold all their land and went to live at Buffalo Creek with the Senecas. The Onondagas and Senecas also saw their landholdings shrink drastically.

Voluntarily, the Iroquois sold most of their land after 1784. They were strongly pressured but were not actually physically coerced as they had been at Fort Stanwix.

For more than a century, the practice of selling land had been familiar to many Iroquois. The offer of large quantities of gifts, including hoes, kettles, axes, domestic animals, cloth, firearms, gunpowder, and other useful items, and the further promise of additional money payments were tempting to Indians who had become dependent upon manufactured items from Europe that made life easier for them. Bribes and lifetime pensions were also sometimes offered to certain leading chiefs as inducements to sell. After the American Revolution, the immediate gain to be derived from land sales was of great importance to many Iroquois, who saw poverty descending upon them as their old way of life was fast disappearing.

But selling their land only made the Iroquois more dependent. As more and more non-Indians settled in the regions bordering on their territory and cleared the land for farming, the game animals moved farther away. Continued land sales thus made hunting more and more difficult for the Iroquois and led them to seek other sources of support. In the short run, everyone profited from the sale of land. In the long run, the Iroquois were selling their birthright and their independence, although they did not realize it at the time. Tiny reservations surrounded by a sea of non-Indians were all that was left of the once vast domain of the Six Nations Confederacy. With their land gone, their once awesome power was but a memory.

The division of the confederacy into Canadian (Grand River) and New York branches after the American Revolution had weakened the old League. Its members were pushed apart by conflicting interests and by their respective relations with either U.S. or British officials. Factional disputes also arose on both sides of the border over League diplomacy and leadership issues. The League became unable to function as a unified whole.

By 1803, the Grand River Iroquois had transferred the council fire of the confederacy to the Onondaga village on their own reserve. The Iroquois on the American side still looked to Buffalo Creek as their capital. The firekeeper there was an Onondaga named Uthawa, or Captain Cold. After Captain Cold's death in 1847, the council fire on the American side was moved back to the Onondaga Reservation in central New York. The League became permanently divided, with a set of chiefs elected for each side of the border.

The political and military decline of the Iroquois Confederacy was accompanied by social decline on the reservations. In earlier times, the men had traveled widely to hunt, fight, and carry on diplomacy. Now the men had very little to do. Hunting was much restricted. The warriors could go to war only when and if they were needed as volunteers in the whites' army. Diplomacy was limited to a few leading men negotiating with representatives of the federal government or occasional embassies traveling to the U.S. capital. Only the women had a secure place in Iroquois society. They continued, as of old, to carry on with their traditional tasks as mothers, housekeepers, and farmers.

The loss of morale and disintegrating conditions on the reservations resulted in idleness, chronic drunkenness, gossip, violent disputes, and family instability. The Iroquois had reached the lowest point in their existence.

Certain non-Indians attempted to help the Iroquois make a transition to their new way of life on the reservation. *Quakers* had been concerned about Indians for more than one hundred years. In 1798, they directed their concern toward the Allegany Seneca living along the New York–Pennsylvania border. Rather than stressing conversion to their particular form of religion, the Quakers sent people to teach reading, writing, and arithmetic and the crafts and skills needed in a modern farming community. As the Quakers put it, they wanted to promote "the works of the handy workman." The Quakers also promoted their concept of morality and ideals of sobriety and a stable family life.

Cornplanter, the chief warrior of the Senecas, had for years been advocating that the Indians adopt the economic system of their non-Indian neighbors, including the idea of men working in agriculture. He therefore firmly supported the Quaker missionaries and their program.

Living in Cornplanter's village at the time was his half-brother, the sachem chief Ganiodaiyo, or Handsome Lake. The chief was a well-known medicine man but was also a chronic and dissipated alcoholic. He took to his bed in May 1799, weakened in body and deathly ill from incessant drinking.

On the morning of June 15, as he was coming out of his cabin, he collapsed and was helped back to bed. The news

This 1905 drawing by Jesse Cornplanter depicts Handsome Lake preaching the "New Religion" or Longhouse Religion as it is known today. Handsome Lake's doctrine ("The Good Word") emphasized the importance of family relations, abstinence from alcohol, and the encouragement of men's participation in the agricultural economy as a way to help reform the lives of the Senecas.

spread fast that Handsome Lake was dying. As his relatives and friends gathered by his bedside, he lay still, showing no signs of life. About half an hour later, the watchers noticed that he seemed to be breathing. Then they felt the beginning of a weak pulse. Finally, after two hours, he opened his eyes. To the wonder of all present, Handsome Lake began to relate a profound religious experience that he had just had.

He had seen a vision, he said. Three finely dressed messengers in ceremonial costume had come to him with a command from the Creator. They told him first that he was to choose his sister and her husband as his medicine persons. Then he was to attend the Strawberry Festival to be held the next day, when the people would give thanks for the ripening of this berry. There, he was to preach the message of *Gaiwiio*, the Good Word. This message was to condemn whiskey, witchcraft, magic love potions of enticement that destroyed families, and the practice of abortion. Wrongdoers must confess and repent of their wickedness. Because Handsome Lake was still too weak to attend the ceremonial himself, Cornplanter preached his brother's message for him.

For the Iroquois, who placed much trust in dreams and visions, this message had a profound impact. It was the first of several visions that would come to Handsome Lake. It also led to the practice of a new religion by his people.

In the following months, Handsome Lake had other visions relating to moral and social reform. During these periods, he went into a trance and saw many wonders and gained much wisdom. He witnessed the punishment of the wicked in hell: drunkards were drinking hot liquid metal; men who had beaten their wives were pounding on a burning female image; gamblers were playing with red-hot metal cards; witches were being dipped into a kettle whose contents boiled over; immoral individuals were suffering burning torments. He also traveled to the realm of the blessed, meeting the spirits of the good people he had known on Earth, and learning in this happy land how families in his own village should live in peace. He was also instructed by the sacred messenger who accompanied him on his journey that Indians should continue to perform their traditional religious ceremonies, particularly the Midwinter Festival.

In yet another vision during a third trance period, Handsome Lake was told to have the Gaiwiio written down in a book to be preserved for all time. He was also instructed to carry the message to all the peoples of the Six Nations.

The Good Word began to bring reformation into the lives of the Senecas, particularly when Handsome Lake combined his religious teachings with an emphasis on loyal and affectionate family relations, abstinence from alcohol, and encouragement of men's participation in the agricultural economy. Handsome Lake's doctrine thus gave religious reinforcement to the social transformation that his brother Cornplanter and the Quakers were promoting.

The Gaiwiio as taught by Handsome Lake gradually spread to other reservations. During his lifetime, it was known as the "New Religion," as distinct from the "Old Religion" of the Iroquois. Handsome Lake's teaching survives today, now known as the "Old Religion" or Longhouse Religion. It is the faith of modern Iroquois traditionalists.

The Quakers were not the only Christian group working among the Iroquois in the nineteenth century. At Caughnawaga and St. Regis, the Catholics continued their missionary tradition. In addition to the Quakers, other Protestants with missionaries on Iroquois reservations included the Episcopalians, Baptists, Methodists, and the New York Missionary Society, an inter-denominational Protestant group. The New York Missionary Society sent pastors and teachers to organize churches and schools on the Tuscarora Reservation in Niagara County and the Buffalo Creek Reservation. Like the Quakers, they stressed men's participation in agriculture and taught such domestic skills as sewing, spinning, and weaving.

The New York Missionary Society later merged with the United Foreign Missionary Society, a largely Presbyterian organization. This, in turn, still later merged with the Boston-based American Board of Commissioners for Foreign Missions, a Congregational church organization. The most noteworthy of the American Board missionaries was Asher Wright, preacher to the Senecas. He served faithfully for many years, not only as a religious teacher but also as a champion and protector of Indian rights. He also devised a writing system for the Seneca language using the English alphabet and edited a newspaper in the Seneca language.

Eleazar Williams, a Caughnawaga Indian who later lived at St. Regis, had settled among the Oneidas in 1816 and began preaching to them as an Episcopalian. He spoke fluent Oneida and was a spellbinding orator. In a short time, he converted most of the Oneidas to the Episcopalian faith. Hoping to establish an Iroquois empire in the west with himself as

Eleazar Williams, a Caughnawaga Indian, converted many Oneidas to the Episcopal religion and tried to entice them to move to Wisconsin Territory in hopes of creating a vast Iroquois empire. Though most Oneidas opposed Williams' plan, a number traveled west in 1823 and settled near Green Bay, Wisconsin, on land purchased from the Menominee and Winnebago Indians.

leader, Williams set forth a plan to sell all Oneida lands in New York and move to Wisconsin Territory. Despite his persuasive powers, Williams' plan met with overwhelming opposition from the Oneidas. He was, however, backed by a few young Oneida warriors. With their support, he gained assistance from some members of Congress and the Ogden Land Company, which had the exclusive right in New York State to buy Iroquois land. Their influence enabled Williams to purchase a large tract of land from the Menominee and Winnebago Indians in Wisconsin. In 1823, those Oneidas who supported the move left their New York land and, with Williams, began the emigration to their new reservation in the west, near Green Bay, Wisconsin.

From 1830 to 1846, the U.S. government had a policy of forcing all eastern Indians to move west of the Mississippi River in order to make their lands available for settlement by non-Indians. In 1831, as a result of this removal policy, the Iroquois of Ohio, mainly the Senecas and Cayugas, sold off their two reservations at Lewistown and Sandusky and moved southwest to Indian Territory (now the state of Oklahoma).

In 1838, the Ogden Land Company used fraud, bribery, alcohol, and forgery to negotiate the Treaty of Buffalo Creek. Despite revelations about the methods by which the treaty was negotiated, its terms were approved by the U.S. Congress. It deprived the Senecas of all their remaining reservations and provided for removal of all New York Iroquois to Kansas. Both the Quakers and Asher Wright, the Senecas' missionary, publicized the fraud and fought for years to nullify the treaty. In 1842, the Allegany and Cattaraugus Reservations were returned to the Senecas, but Buffalo Creek and Tonawanda remained lost. In 1857, after a long struggle, the Tonawanda Senecas were able to repurchase most of their reservation from the Ogden Land Company.

This would be the end of the assault on Iroquois lands until well into the next century. From the 1940s on, however, both New York State and the federal government would again begin confiscating large areas of the remaining reservations, this time for "public improvements": a dam, a reservoir, roads, and an enlarged waterway.

By the mid-nineteenth century, the program of educating the Iroquois Indians in the ways of non-Indians was beginning to benefit them. Iroquois men were developing small but prosperous farms and were learning other practical skills, such as carpentry. Children and even some adults were beginning to learn the basics of reading, writing, and arithmetic, making them more knowledgeable in their business dealings with non-Indians. A few of the brightest Indian students were able to attend high-quality local private schools off the reservations. Some were even able to go to college.

The Iroquois—particularly the Oneidas—were quite successful in acculturating to white-dominated society. Through their use of fine china, silverware, and other Euro-American-made items, they developed a society that in many ways resembled that of the whites who were nonetheless trying to destroy them. In fact, as early as the colonial period, the Oneidas were making major changes to better fit in with white culture. As a result, when George Washington's forces devastated Iroquois country in 1779 during the American Revolution, they were destroying a society that was actually very similar to their own.

One of the most remarkable of these young educated Indians was a Tonawanda Seneca named Ely S. Parker. Because of his education and his knowledge of English, the chiefs chose him as interpreter when they negotiated with New York State and U.S. officials. While browsing in an Albany bookstore on one of his diplomatic visits to the state capital, Parker met Lewis Henry Morgan, a young lawyer from Aurora, New York. This chance meeting would grow into a lifelong friendship, changing the course of both men's lives. (For additional information on Parker, enter "Ely Parker" into any search engine and browse the many sites listed.)

Morgan had already been interested in the Iroquois and their customs and was therefore delighted to meet this sixteen-year-old Seneca. In future years, Parker served as Morgan's main informant, educating him on Iroquois customs and traditions. Parker also introduced Morgan to the elders and ritualists of the Senecas—people who were more knowledgeable than he about Iroquois customs. Morgan was the first to combine direct observation, in-depth interviewing, and the application of rigorous methods of scholarship to the study of another society's way of life. As a result of his study and research, Morgan wrote a number of articles and books on the Iroquois. Because of his great contribution, Morgan is often called "the father of American *anthropology*."

Ely Parker later studied law but was denied the right to practice because, as an Indian, he was not recognized as a U.S. citizen. Morgan then helped him to get a job with the builders of the Genesee Valley Canal, where he learned engineering. When the American Civil War broke out in 1861, Parker enlisted in the Union Army and rose to become a brigadier general. He served on General Ulysses S. Grant's staff and, because of his fine handwriting, became Grant's military secretary. It was Parker who wrote out the document of surrender that Confederate General Robert E. Lee signed at Appomattox Court House in April 1865. After Grant became president in 1869, Parker became commissioner of Indian Affairs—the first Indian to serve in that post.

The Iroquois studies begun by Lewis Henry Morgan encouraged others to do research on these Indians. As a result, the Iroquois have become one of the most studied and written-about Indian tribal groups in the country. A number of Iroquois themselves have taken lifelong scholarly interest in their own culture and history. The best known of these are Arthur C. Parker, Ely S. Parker's grandnephew, and John N. B. Hewitt, a Tuscarora. Arthur Parker had a long and distinguished career first as an archaeologist with the New York State Museum in Albany and then as director of the Rochester Museum. Hewitt's career was equally distinguished. He was for many years an ethnologist at the Smithsonian Institution

Wolf clan mask, c. 1775. One of the earliest False Faces, this mask is said to have belonged to Joseph Brant.

Onondaga harvest mask, c. 1870. Masks like this one are an important part of Iroquois curing rituals and religious ceremonies.

Seneca living mask (Shayodiowe gowa). Before carvings could be performed, sacred tobacco was burned as an offering to the tree.

Pottery vessel, c. 1500. This St. Lawrence Iroquoian vessel is typical in shape of other Iroquoian pottery, but it is distinguished by the punctates that cover its outer shell.

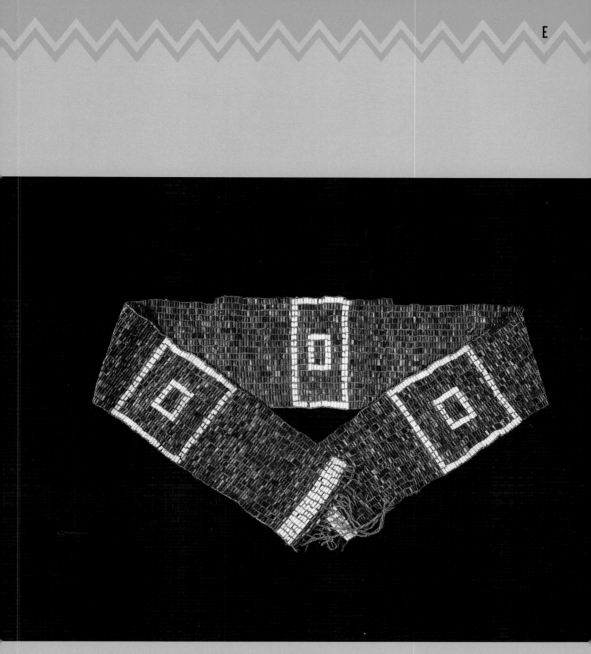

Wampum belts similar to this one were used by the Iroquois to record important historical events and stand as records of negotiations and treaties. Wampum is derived from the Algonquian word *wampumpeag*, meaning "white (bead) strings," and is made from clam shells.

The Iroquois have sought to protect and preserve relics from their past, including cultural remains such as these that were unearthed in Hamburg, New York, and secured for repatriation.

By the nineteenth century, Iroquois beadwork had caught the fancy of European and American tourists who visited New York State. Such souvenir trinkets as this "Beaded Whimsy," c. 1900, were sold to visitors.

This sculpture, which is housed in the Carnegie Museum of Natural History in Pittsburgh, Pennsylvania, depicts some of the animals that represent Iroquois clans. The Mohawk and the Oneida tribes were represented by the turtle, wolf, and bear, while, in addition to the aforementioned animals, the Onondaga, Cayuga, and Seneca tribes were represented by the snipe, heron, beaver, deer, eel, and hawk.

in Washington, D.C., and published an enormous amount of scholarly material on the Iroquois.

The Longhouse traditionalists still living on today's reservations and the Iroquois scholars of past years have done much to keep alive knowledge of the language, history, and customs of the People of the Extended Lodge. The traditionalists and scholars both have preserved a precious heritage for the generations who will follow them.

8

The Modern Iroquois

As the nineteenth century progressed, the Iroquois made a successful transition from female-practiced to male-practiced agriculture. Other customs began to change as well. In the old days, the Iroquois had lived in bark longhouses, each of which contained an expanded or extended family. That usually meant an older married woman with her married daughters, their husbands, and their children. Iroquois women, as the farmers, had always played a key role in the traditional community economy. The land belonged to them. With the growing predominance of male-practiced agriculture, it became the tendency to move into separate family houses built in non-Indian style. The smaller, male-dominated family (father, mother, and children) now became the normal Iroquois pattern, the same as it was among rural non-Indians.

Land, once the possession of the women, now became the possession of men as it was bought and sold by male farmers.

The Iroquois had traditionally lived in longhouses (pictured here), where several families cohabitated due to the matrilineal line of descent. But by the nineteenth century, the Iroquois had largely moved into separate family houses as the men began to farm and own land and subsequently became the head of household.

Although all reservation land belonged to the nation inhabiting that reservation and could not legally be sold to non-Indians, the Iroquois began to accept the right of private ownership of the soil by individuals or families and the right of inheritance of land. Individual Iroquois who owned land they did not or could not farm sometimes rented it out to other Indians or even to non-Indian farmers. In many ways, the Iroquois in the nineteenth century were approaching the patriarchal (male-dominated) social system of their non-Indian neighbors.

In 1848, the Senecas of the Cattaraugus and Allegany Reservations had a quiet revolution. These Senecas had become very dissatisfied over the way the chiefs dispensed the annuity payments that came to them from the federal government as a result of the 1794 Treaty of Canandaigua between the United States and the Six Nations on the U.S. side of the border. These annuities consisted of a yearly payment of $4,500, largely in trade goods. The payments were to be apportioned among those tribal groups living in New York State that had signed the treaty.

Most of these New York Senecas wanted the payments made directly to the heads of families, rather than having the chiefs take a portion out first for general governmental expenses on the reservations. Also, the people still harbored grievances against the chiefs for signing the Treaty of Buffalo Creek in 1838, which had deprived them of a tremendous amount of land. As a result, they overthrew the hereditary chiefs and set up an elective councillor system under a written constitution. Henceforth, these two reservations would be known as the Seneca Nation. In imitation of the governing system of their non-Indian neighbors, the Seneca Nation deprived its women of the right to vote. It was not until 1964 that the women of the Seneca Nation secured the right to vote in tribal elections.

The Tonawanda Senecas, who had never recognized the Treaty of Buffalo Creek, retained their original form of government, with hereditary chiefs chosen by the senior women of each clan. These two divisions in government exist to this day between the Seneca Nation (Allegany and Cattaraugus) and the more traditionalist Tonawanda Band of Senecas.

The St. Regis Mohawk Reservation was located both south and north of the St. Lawrence River, in New York State and in the provinces of Quebec and Ontario in Canada. The Mohawks on the U.S. side had adopted an elective system of government in 1802. Originally, there were three elected "trustees." Later, this number was expanded to twelve, and the elected officials were called chiefs.

In the twentieth century, the Longhouse Religion of Handsome Lake was established on the Caughnawaga Reservation in the 1920s and on the St. Regis Reservation in the 1930s. This religious group has revived the old hereditary chief system and, on both reservations, these chiefs now exist in opposition to the elective chiefs who govern the reserves.

The Six Nations Reserve in Canada had maintained a hereditary chief system throughout the nineteenth century. The Canadian government, however, imposed a *patrilineal* form of descent (according to the father's family line) on all Indian groups in Canada. To the *matrilineal* Iroquois (descent is traced through the mother's family line), this has caused no end of confusion, for it affects tribal membership and even throws clan membership into doubt.

In 1924, as a result of a political upheaval on the Six Nations Reserve, an elective council was established. It is currently the recognized form of government. The hereditary chiefs appointed by clan mothers continue to function, largely in a ritual capacity connected with the various longhouses of the Handsome Lake religion on the reserve. In 1959 and again in 1970, the hereditary chiefs' faction and their followers attempted to seize control of the reservation government but failed.

Today, only three reservations—Onondaga, Tonawanda, and Tuscarora—all in New York, are governed by the traditional system of hereditary chiefs. The clan mothers of the respective tribal clans still nominate the chiefs for their clan, and these men are then raised to office by means of the ancient Condolence Council.

The Oneidas of Wisconsin lost a tremendous amount of land as a result of the General Allotment Act of 1887. This legislation was an attempt by the U.S. government to destroy the tribal form of society in the West, by breaking up the reservations into small parcels of land that were then given, or allotted, to individual Indians. The Indians were to become farmers and citizens and thus more readily assimilate into the general population. Once their land had been taken out of federal protective status and given to them for private ownership, however, the Oneidas were unable to pay the local and county taxes that were levied on these allotments. As a result, they saw almost all of their reservation land taken away from them. Their tribal government also fell apart.

Indians continued to lose their land as a result of the General Allotment Act until there was a change in government policy in the late 1920s and 1930s. The Indian Reorganization Act of 1934 was of particular importance in beginning to solve the Wisconsin Oneidas' problems. They took advantage of the provisions of this law to form a new government, write a constitution, and incorporate the tribe. Under their new government, Oneida men and women both could vote and hold political office. The federal government also repurchased some additional land for the tribe.

The Indian Reorganization Act was a new beginning for the Oneidas. They established a number of business enterprises on the Wisconsin reservation and have also built a home for their senior citizens and the Oneida Museum to preserve their heritage. Today, their leaders are well educated and capable, and after many years of struggle, the community has begun to prosper.

Whether in Wisconsin, Oklahoma, New York, Quebec, or Ontario, most reservation Iroquois today live in much the same way as neighboring rural non-Indians do. Although many still maintain vegetable gardens for their own use, most Iroquois are no longer farmers. The small amount of land they possess and the large financial outlay needed for modern farm machinery put full-time farming beyond the means of most Iroquois. The men today prefer construction work and factory employment and usually commute daily from their reservations to work. They are particularly noted as ironworkers, traveling throughout the United States to construct skyscrapers and bridges. Women also often work off the reservation in a variety of occupations.

Many Iroquois have permanently moved to the cities where employment is available. The largest nonreservation Iroquois populations in New York State cities are in Buffalo, Niagara

Falls, Rochester, and the borough of Brooklyn in New York City, where many St. Regis and Caughnawaga people have moved. Many Oneidas live in Milwaukee, Wisconsin.

An increasing number of young Iroquois men and women complete high school and go on to colleges and universities, where they often study such professions as teaching, social work, law, and medicine. A few Iroquois have also gone into state and federal government service, some reaching high-level posts. In 1966, Robert L. Bennett, an Oneida from Wisconsin, was appointed commissioner of Indian Affairs. He was followed in that post from 1969 to 1972 by Louis R. Bruce, Jr., of St. Regis Mohawk and Oglala Sioux ancestry.

During much of the twentieth century, the Iroquois have suffered continual attacks on their rights, their independence, and their land holdings. One such denial of their rights followed passage of the Immigration Act of 1924. One section of this act stated: "No alien ineligible to citizenship shall be admitted to the United States." Because of American prejudices during the period, this provision was specifically intended to keep Asians out of the country. Immigration officials also applied the ban to Indians who were attempting to cross the border from Canada. Because so many Indians had been accustomed to crossing the border freely to visit friends and family and to work, this policy came as a serious blow. Concerned Iroquois fought this interpretation of the act on both moral and legal grounds.

Jay's Treaty of 1794 between the United States and Great Britain had specifically permitted "the Indians dwelling on either side of said boundary line, freely to pass and repass" into each country. Paul K. Diabo, a Caughnawaga Mohawk who was now prevented from coming into the United States to work at his usual job, hired a Philadelphia law firm to fight his case for him. Clinton Rickard, a Tuscarora living on the Tuscarora Reservation near Niagara Falls, fought the Immigration Act by informing sympathetic non-Indians about the effects of the

In 1966, Robert L. Bennett, an Oneida from Wisconsin, was appointed the first commissioner of Indian Affairs. In 1969, Bennett, along with John C. Rainer, established American Indian Scholarships (AIS) to help Native Americans obtain professional degrees. Now known as the American Indian Graduate Center (AIGC), it remains the only national nonprofit organization dedicated to aiding Indian graduate students in all fields of study.

law, forming the Indian Defense League of America with other concerned Indians in 1926, and lobbying Congress. Diabo's and Rickard's efforts eventually succeeded. The courts recognized the supremacy of Jay's Treaty, and Congress in 1928 specifically provided for uninterrupted Indian passage over the border.

The Indian Defense League of America is the oldest ongoing Indian rights group in the United States and continues to fight injustice against Indians. It also preserves a special celebration held every year on the third Saturday in July. The Border Crossing Celebration commemorates the victory gained in 1928. "Border Crossing" has become a general Indian Day in the Niagara Falls area, where Indians from the cities and reservations gather in colorful costumes for a parade across the border and a picnic at a nearby park, with sports, speeches by dignitaries, displays of Indian dancing, the sale of Indian crafts, and general assertions of pride in being Indian. (For additional information on this organization, enter "Indian Defense League of America" into any search engine and browse the many sites listed.)

Shortly after World War II, in the late 1940s and 1950s, the U.S. government attempted to end its involvement in Indian affairs. This meant the end of federal responsibility for Indians, removal of Indian lands from federal trust status, and nullification, or *termination*, of the many treaties with the various Indian tribes. The plan included a *relocation* program by which the Bureau of Indian Affairs (BIA) urged Indians throughout the country to leave the reservations and move to cities. BIA officials offered every Indian a one-way ticket to a city where the BIA had an office that could help the newcomer find housing and work. The object was to move as many Indians as possible off the reservations and eventually to close down the bureau itself. The government called this policy "freeing the Indians." Under this program, the government terminated federally recognized status for 109 Indian groups. The termination program succeeded primarily in "freeing" the Indians from their land and plunging them deeper into poverty.

The New York Iroquois united in a vigorous struggle to fight termination. They partially succeeded. The federal treaties with the Iroquois still stand, but civil and criminal legal jurisdiction over the Iroquois has been turned over to New York State. The Oneidas of Wisconsin and the Senecas-Cayugas of Oklahoma also fought doggedly against the termination of their status and were eventually successful.

The next attacks were waged against Iroquois land, and the Iroquois consistently lost. In the 1950s, the Army Corps of Engineers, over the strong objection of the Senecas, proposed to build a dam near Warren, Pennsylvania, for flood-control purposes. When completed, the Kinzua Dam would flood the entire Cornplanter Reservation in Pennsylvania and large sections of the Allegany Reservation in New York. The building of this dam would have thus been in violation of the Treaty of Canandaigua of 1794 in which the United States guaranteed the Iroquois safe possession of their land.

The Senecas conducted a major campaign against the dam through the newspapers and television, in the courts, and by lobbying Congress and Pennsylvania and New York State officials. They gained the support of many non-Indian religious and civil liberties organizations as well as that of other Indian nations across the country. Cornelius Seneca, George Heron, and Basil Williams, each of whom served as president of the Seneca Nation at various times during these years of struggle, led their people in a determined battle to preserve their land.

The Seneca Nation hired Dr. Arthur E. Morgan as consulting engineer. Morgan, who had formerly headed the Tennessee Valley Authority (TVA), worked with Barton M. Jones, who had been the chief designing engineer of that vast flood-control project. They drew up an alternate plan that would be more effective for flood control and would preserve Indian lands. The Army Corps of Engineers was uninterested in Morgan's plan and the government went ahead with the construction of the Kinzua Dam.

The completed dam resulted in the flooding of more than 9,000 acres of Seneca land, necessitating the removal of 130 Seneca families and the relocation of Seneca graves to a safe location. This disruption of their lives caused profound shock to the Senecas. Even today, those who went through this shattering experience cannot speak of it without deep emotion and overwhelming grief.

The government compensated the Seneca Nation financially for the loss of their land. The Senecas put the money to good use by building two community centers—one on each reserve—and setting up a scholarship fund. But to the Senecas, their land was far more important. Land is forever, but money is soon gone.

Between 1958 and 1960, the Tuscaroras fought an attempt by the New York State Power Authority to confiscate a large portion of their reservation near Niagara Falls for a reservoir. Considering their land more valuable than money, the chiefs' council, under Chief Elton Greene, turned down a large monetary offer and instead took the case through the legal system all the way to the U.S. Supreme Court. While the case was still pending in the courts, the State Power Authority sent personnel onto the reservation to begin work. The men and women of the tribe united in a militant mass obstruction of this invasion, standing in front of surveyors' stakes, lying down in front of trucks, carrying protest signs, and engaging in heated arguments with the workers. One fourteen-year-old boy took his rifle and shot a stake out of a surveyor's hand, demonstrating the skill that Indian men and boys continue to develop as hunters even in modern times. The State Power Authority then called in well-armed police to protect them as they dug up the reservation.

On March 7, 1960, the Supreme Court rendered a split decision of 4−3 against the Tuscaroras. The Tuscaroras had lost, but both they and their cause had received wide publicity throughout the country. The militant demonstrations they had carried on for months while their case was pending in the courts were the beginning of a new tactic in Indian protest movements. This method would be utilized by other Indians across the country in future years.

The Caughnawaga and St. Regis Reservations also suffered significant land losses when the St. Lawrence Seaway was enlarged in the late 1950s. Both Canada and the United States ignored treaties and Indian land rights in the interest of industrial development. These governments' idea of progress had little room for Indians.

During the latter half of the twentieth century, however, there were some Iroquois legal victories that promised more justice in the future for Indians. In 1942, the Seneca Nation won a lawsuit in the U.S. Court of Appeals for the Second Circuit of New York against non-Indian leaseholders on the Allegany Reservation. In the mid-nineteenth century, many whites had been moving illegally onto the reservation and had established some all-white communities, notably the city of Salamanca. Over time, these newcomers began leasing the lands they occupied from either the Seneca council or from individual Senecas. The U.S. Congress then confirmed the leases in 1875. These annual rentals were very low, even by nineteenth-century standards. Some were less than ten dollars a year, and some were as low as one dollar a year. Eventually, many non-Indian leaseholders considered the rentals so inconsequential that they ceased paying them at all. After the 1942 legal decision in their favor, the Seneca Nation began eviction proceedings against these leaseholders who still refused to honor their arrears payments and current rents. Both federal and state courts refused to hear appeals from the delinquent lease-holders. By 1944, new and higher leases were then negotiated by the Seneca Nation, settling this longstanding grievance.

In 1974, the U.S. Supreme Court gave the Oneida Nation of New York access to the federal courts to pursue their claims for lands taken from them by illegal state treaties in the late eighteenth and early nineteenth centuries that did not have the required federal commissioners present. In 1985, the Oneidas won a test case in the Supreme Court for unlawful seizure of the lands they had once held in what later became Oneida and Madison Counties in the state. This decision upheld the Oneidas' right to further pursue their longstanding land claim.

It is often difficult for non-Indians to understand the deep attachment Indians feel for their land. For the Iroquois, their reservations are the only lands they have retained as their own after years of pressure to separate them from the millions of acres that were once theirs. Preservation of their current land-holdings, with relatively few acres left, means the preservation of their communities, their heritage, and their identity. The reservations are home: the place where Indians can be themselves, practice their customs, their religion, and their way of life. Upon their own land, among their own people, the Iroquois are most truly themselves. Even those who live in the cities return frequently to the reservation to visit relatives and friends and to be spiritually refreshed.

In their own communities, the Iroquois retain their sovereignty and their independence. They can govern themselves and preserve their own sense of worth. Even though they have lived for nearly two hundred years in close proximity to non-Indians, they have preserved their attachment to Indian values. They take from outsiders what is of benefit to them, what will make their lives better; but most Iroquois have no desire to assimilate and thus lose their own unique identity. They are proud of who they are and proud of being contemporary representatives of the Kanonghsionni, the Extended Lodge of the Iroquois Founding Fathers.

9

The Iroquois Today and Tomorrow

T he loss of vast quantities of their land in the last half of the twentieth century aroused in the Iroquois a sense of nationalism, militancy, and determination to oppose the continuing high-handed treatment by the white-dominated government. They had tried using the court system to preserve their land but the courts had repeatedly ruled against them. The Senecas, in particular, had relied on the 1794 Treaty of Canandaigua, which had guaranteed them possession of their land in perpetuity. The U.S. Congress ignored that treaty's promise and overruled it by giving permission for the building of the Kinzua Dam, which flooded all of the Cornplanter Reservation in Pennsylvania and large portions of the Allegany Reservation along the southern tier of New York State. The Mohawks of Caughnawaga and St. Regis, who lived along the St. Lawrence River, would also futilely seek help from the courts in Canada and the United States but would also resort to militant demonstrations against the intruders on their lands. The Caughnawaga Reserve near Montreal lost more land to the St. Lawrence Seaway Project than did St. Regis, but it was at the latter community where some of the most important protests took place. The determined public demonstrations in defense of their lands by both the Tuscaroras and the Mohawks were widely publicized in the press in both the United States and Canada and marked a new phase in Iroquois history in which the unity and sovereignty of the Iroquois people was emphasized.

The St. Regis Reservation, which its residents prefer to call by its Mohawk name, *Akwesasne* ("Where the Partridge Drums"), spans the international border between the United States and Canada. Parts of the reservation are in New York, Ontario, and Quebec. The Cornwall Island portion of the reservation, where a significant number of the Mohawk population lives, is in the middle of the St. Lawrence River and is on the Ontario side of the border. This island came under particular pressure from the St. Lawrence Seaway Project as the Seaway Authority, without permission from the resident Mohawks, designated 130 acres of the land for new highway access to the International Bridge, which crossed the island and connected Ontario with New York State.

In the fall of 1959, Chief John Sharrow, himself a resident of Cornwall Island, demanded that the St. Lawrence Seaway Authority pay the Mohawks $45,000 for three years' rental for the new road on Indian-owned land. If the Authority refused, Sharrow warned that his people would block the bridge to traffic. When the Seaway Authority objected, the Mohawks announced that they planned to collect a fifty-cent toll from each car that used the new road. The Authority then gave in and paid the requested rental fee.

In late 1968, however, the Mohawks on Cornwall Island were faced with another threat to their rights as Indians when Canadian customs collectors began to require them to pay customs duties on all purchased items brought onto the island, including food, if the items were worth more than five dollars. This was a violation of the 1794 Jay's Treaty between the United States and Great Britain. Article III of that treaty had permitted Indians to cross the border with goods that were customarily used by Indians. The Treaty of Ghent in 1814 had reaffirmed that right. Canada had refused to recognize Jay's Treaty, saying that it had never been approved or implemented by Canadian law.

Cornwall Island was and is an Indian reservation, part of the St. Regis (Akwesasne) Reservation. The Mohawks contended that they were still in their own country when they traveled from one part of their territory to another, and they refused to recognize the whites' international boundary as separating their country.

To make their point, the Mohawks secretly began to plan a massive protest against the levying of customs duties. On December 18, 1968, they began a huge blockade of the International Bridge. With their bodies and their automobiles blocking the roadway, they brought bridge traffic to a standstill. The Royal Canadian Mounted Police and the Ontario Provincial Police were called out and arrested forty-one demonstrators. Various local and national newspapers sent reporters and national television stations to broadcast the incident in both Canada and the United States, giving the Mohawks and their cause wide publicity.

After continued discussions, another bridge blockage in February 1969, and more negotiations, the Mohawks at last won their objective. The Canadian government finally agreed not to charge the local Mohawks customs duties.

As a result of the struggles for Indian rights at St. Regis, the Indian newspaper *Akwesasne Notes* came into being. At first, it was composed mainly of reproduced clippings from various non-Indian newspapers regarding the Mohawks' efforts to preserve their homeland. Later, it began to include original commentary and letters to the editor, and it eventually emerged as an important national Indian newspaper.

Also, since July 1983, the Akwesasne community has been publishing the newspaper *Indian Time* to give the people of their nation not only news of their own community but of their sister Iroquois nations as well.

An important educational endeavor also arose from this protest era of the late 1960s. Akwesasne Mohawk Ernest Benedict, who lived on Cornwall Island, planned a far-reaching project that he named the North American Indian Travelling College. The proposed institution would acquire its own library of Indian-related literature and would be staffed by volunteer teachers who were knowledgeable in Indian rituals and traditions. Using vans, the college would visit Indian reserves, especially in Canada, giving residents general information on Indians of the Americas, on Indian traditions and culture, Indian history, achievement, sovereignty, and treaty rights. The object of the college was to bring the Indian communities in Canada together and to promote the unity of Indian peoples. Nothing like this had ever been tried before. The success of the Traveling College is marked by its staying power: it was created in 1968 and is still active in the twenty-first century. Throughout its existence, the Travelling College has had a strong educational impact on Indians in Canada.

A further building block in the foundation establishing Iroquois sovereignty in this modern age was the Onondaga dispute with the New York State Department of Transportation in 1971. The state, without consulting the Onondagas, had planned to widen a section of Interstate 81 that ran along the border of the Onondaga Reservation and create an acceleration lane that would take far more land than was agreeable to the reservation residents. In 1952, the Onondaga chiefs had granted an easement of approximately 89 acres of their land for this portion of the road in exchange for a $31,500 payment to their nation, but they had not agreed to future extensive additions to the highway. In August, the Onondagas, who were joined by a number of volunteers from the Mohawk, Oneida, and Tuscarora Nations, organized a sit-down on the work site, which stopped construction on the road. The protest grew larger over the weeks, continuing on through October until an agreement was reached between Governor Nelson Rockefeller and the council of chiefs, allowing the state, as a safety measure, to widen the shoulder of the highway but not to include the large acceleration lane that had originally been planned. All the arrests made during the demonstration were also dismissed. It was noteworthy that the governor of New York had negotiated on an equal basis with the Onondaga chiefs and had reached an agreeable compromise.

The Supreme Court cases in 1974 and 1985 would also open the door for Iroquois nations to receive justice for lands illegally taken from them in the 1790s and early 1800s by New York State. Both New York State and the U.S. government had for years blocked Iroquois attempts either to secure payment for lands illegally purchased or to receive compensatory territory for lands taken in the past. Past Iroquois attempts at legal redress had been blocked by a series of legal maneuvers. It was claimed that either the events were so old that the law had gone by the boards, that the appeal was in the wrong court, or that the case should go instead to the Indian Claims Commission, which, in turn, would always deny the claim. The Bureau of Indian Affairs also took no initiative to help Iroquois claimants.

The U.S. Nonintercourse Acts of 1790 and 1793 had forbidden purchases of Indian lands without the presence of a U.S. commissioner at the proceedings. New York had ignored these laws in carrying out most of its land purchases from Indians after 1793. There was, however, a problem in suing a state. The Eleventh Amendment to the U.S. Constitution protects states from being sued by "citizens of another state, or by citizens or subjects of any foreign state." The lawyer for the Oneida Nation was also aware that the Eleventh Amendment had been interpreted to bar federal court jurisdiction over lawsuits for damages against a state. This amendment, however, says nothing about not suing a county.

As a way around the Eleventh Amendment protection for a state, the Oneidas' lawyer instead sued Madison and Oneida counties in New York. Included as petitioners in this suit were the Oneida Indian Nation of New York and the Oneida Indian Nation of Wisconsin, both of whose ancestors had been living in New York during the 1790s and early 1800s. The case worked its way through the lower federal courts and was finally decided in favor of the Oneidas in the U.S. Supreme Court on January 21, 1974. This had been a test case to determine whether the Oneidas had a right to sue for land loss. The Supreme Court concluded that they did have "a current right to possession conferred by federal law, wholly independent of state law."

The decision overturned a century of legal defeats for Indian claimants and freed the Oneidas to pursue their land claims further in federal court. Also, because of this legal victory, other Indian nations now could pursue their own land claims.

The second Oneida case was decided by the U.S. Supreme Court on March 4, 1985. Not only were the Oneida Indian Nation of New York and the Oneida Indian Nation of Wisconsin included as petitioners, but also the Oneida of the Thames Band Council, whose ancestors had migrated to Ontario, Canada, after 1839. The Court decided that Indian nations have a common-law right to seek legal redress in the federal courts for recovery of lands to recompense for lands illegally taken from them.

The Oneidas' success encouraged other Iroquois nations that had lost lands in New York to bring suit in federal court.

Both the Cayuga and the Seneca Nations would now petition the federal courts in lawsuits against New York State.

The Cayugas had lost their entire land holdings in New York in 1795 as a result of state purchase. In a trial in the U.S. District Court for the Northern District of New York in January 2000, a jury determined that the lands occupied by the Cayugas in 1795 were worth $37.8 million. A second trial before a judge was held in the summer of 2000 to determine the damage due the Cayugas for not having had control of their lands since 1795. In a decision reached on October 2, 2001, the judge ruled that an additional $211 million was due the petitioners: the Cayuga Nation of New York and the Seneca-Cayuga Tribe of Oklahoma. New York State appealed the decision to a higher court.

The Seneca Nation of Indians and the Tonawanda Band of Seneca, supported by the U.S. government, brought suit in the U.S. District Court for the Western District of New York against New York State for loss of Grand Island in the Niagara River. The Senecas lost the case on June 21, 2002, and appealed to a higher federal court. (For additional information on these land claims, enter "Iroquois land claims against New York" into any search engine and browse the many sites listed.)

Presently, the following Iroquois nations have land claims pending against New York State:

Oneida Nation of New York
Oneida Nation of Indians of Wisconsin
Oneida of the Thames Band Council
Cayuga Nation of New York
Seneca-Cayuga Tribe of Oklahoma
Stockbridge-Munsee Band of Mohican Indians
    of Wisconsin
Seneca Nation of Indians
Tonawanda Band of Seneca
St. Regis Mohawks

For well over a century, and particularly in the nineteenth century, the U.S. government had followed a policy of assimilation, often forced assimilation, for American Indians. As the twentieth century drew to a close, it became evident that American Indians were not only *not* going to disappear and become absorbed into the general population, but that they did not *want* to disappear as Indians. The Iroquois, long surrounded by the dominant culture, nonetheless had demonstrated that, although they could work and be friendly with their non-Indian neighbors, they were not willing to abandon their identity, their sovereignty, their history, or their treaty rights. As a result of the militant demonstrations to preserve their land, a new assertiveness arose among them, along with a determination to right old wrongs and to demonstrate pride in being both Indian and Iroquois.

The Iroquois were now living with a renewed sense of their own history and traditions and the value of their culture. Their new concerns included the honoring and preservation of Iroquois lifeways, protecting the remains of their ancient ancestors from archaeological excavations, and retrieving national and sacred objects from museums. The Iroquois took a new interest in improving the education of their young people. They also sought to include their own tribal histories and culture in the school curriculum, along with the teaching of the Iroquois languages.

For all Iroquois people, the education of their children is of great importance. Their young people are considered to be the future of the Iroquois nations. The hopes and aspirations of the parents and their children have not, however, always been met by the schools that Indians attend.

When Iroquois schoolchildren were bussed off the reservation to enter largely non-Indian consolidated schools, they often felt as though they had entered a foreign country. Their teachers and non-Indian classmates often had no knowledge or appreciation of Indian history and culture.

The Iroquois have longed protested that museums have unlawfully held their religious articles and wampum strings and belts, which were traditionally used in treaty negotiations, various ceremonies, and to mark historical records. Although the state of New York passed a bill in 1971 permitting the return of five of the eleven wampum belts housed in the New York State Museum, it wasn't until 1989 that all eleven belts were returned to the Onondagas, who are the keepers of the wampum.

Because of the expense of running small rural Indian schools, the New York Education Department had shut down all but three Iroquois schools by 1965 and was bussing the Indian children off the reservation to nearby consolidated schools. Only the reservation schools at Tuscarora, Onondaga, and Akwesasne (St. Regis) remained open. The plan was to eliminate the grades in those schools gradually and finally to close them down, too, transferring all Indian elementary students to off-reservation schools.

In the late 1960s and early 1970s, Iroquois leaders and parents began to express dissatisfaction with the status of their schools and suggested programs for reforming the curriculum.

By the early 1970s, under pressure from the Tuscarora chiefs and with final approval from the New York Education Department, the Tuscarora language was being taught to children in the Tuscarora school. In later years, an Iroquois culture teacher was also added.

In 1968, the Mohawk at St. Regis (Akwesasne) staged a boycott of the Salmon River School District to protest what they considered inadequate attention to the educational needs of the Indian children at the reservation school. An additional grievance was the fact that the Salmon River Central School District had received special funding designated for "Indian education" but instead had used it for general educational purposes.

In 1971, the Onondagas drew their children out of the Lafayette School District in a similar protest, emphasizing the inadequacy of an educational system that was leading to high dropout rates among Onondaga students. They also complained of lack of cultural enrichment courses for their children, including Onondaga language instruction.

The New York State Education authorities heard these protests and responded favorably. It was agreed to expand the Onondaga school from kindergarten to grade eight. Future Indian language and culture courses were approved. Plans to close the three remaining Iroquois elementary schools were abandoned.

The Regents of the State of New York had finally reversed the state's former policy and had recognized that attempts at forced assimilation of Indians into American society were wrong. At last, the state agreed officially that Indian people should be permitted to retain whatever they wished from their tribal cultures and to adopt from American culture whatever was of greatest value to their needs. In both New York State and Wisconsin, the Iroquois nations have been taking a leading role in improving both the educational facilities and the educational opportunities for their young people.

The Wisconsin Oneidas had for many years been sending their children to off-reservation schools for the duration of their education. With the arrival of President Lyndon Johnson's "Great Society" program in the 1960s, however, the Oneidas saw an opportunity to benefit their people, particularly in the area of early childhood education. They took advantage of funding from Head Start programs to open an Early Childhood Center on the reservation. This preschool program has proved enormously helpful in developing basic skills in young children and also in providing them with an early knowledge of their culture and the Oneida language.

An adult education program was also started at Oneida to provide a means for older members of the community who had never finished high school to upgrade their education and to encourage the younger generation to complete high school. The General Education Diploma (GED) is awarded to those who complete the course of study.

One of the very unique educational programs that the Wisconsin Oneidas have established in their community is the Oneida Tribal School. This is an alternative school, similar to public school in that it provides basic reading, writing, arithmetic, and other general studies, but different in that it teaches students their tribal culture, history, and Oneida language. Parents are free to choose whether to send their children to an off-reservation public school or to the Tribal School.

Senecas in New York, like other Iroquois groups, have sought both to preserve Iroquois lifeways and to improve the education of their children so that these young people will be able to succeed in the modern world while still valuing their own culture. In pursuit of this goal, the Senecas have obtained both federal and state funds and have also used their own revenue to establish early childhood education programs on their reservations. They know that quality education in the very early years is fundamental to successful learning in later years. The Tonawanda Senecas have a Lifeways Program for pre-kindergarten through second grade, teaching general courses as well as Seneca language and culture.

The Seneca Nation (Cattaraugus and Allegany) has used its own funds to build two fine modern school buildings, one for each territory. Each Early Childhood Center has both a day-school program and an afterschool program, which are identical at both schools. The day school serves children from age six weeks to five years, and has special programs for infants, toddlers, Head Start students, and pre-kindergarten. Children of kindergarten age through age twelve go to public schools, either at Gowanda (Cattaraugus) or Salamanca (Allegany). These older children then go to their respective Seneca Nation schools for a variety of afterschool programs, which can include arts and crafts, help with homework, Seneca language instruction, and field trips. Teachers in these Nation schools are paid entirely with Seneca Nation funds, except for the Head Start teachers, who are paid with federal funds. Cattaraugus, which has a larger population than Allegany, has recently enlarged its building in order to accommodate a waiting list of children.

At Allegany, there is also a Faithkeeper's School, which has some similarities to the Tribal School in Oneida, Wisconsin, but is a private parochial school that teaches both the traditional Longhouse Religion as well as Seneca history, culture, and the Seneca language. The children presently attending range in age from six to fourteen.

The school was founded in 2000 by a husband and wife team, Dar and Sandy Dowdy. Originally, it met in a three-room log house. As the program progressed, one Seneca businessman, impressed by the accomplishments of the school, donated a generous sum of money to cover the cost of constructing a large, modern, roomy building. The new schoolhouse was ready for use in 2003.

Dar Dowdy explained his motivation in starting the school: "Our strong focus is to preserve and maintain the traditional Seneca language, which is the means [by which] we carry on our ancient Seneca customs, ceremonies, history and laws. It has been this way through the centuries. Through the means of handing it down orally to generations of Seneca people, our customs and traditions have remained alive and constant. Now, it is time to teach our children the language and the culture so this knowledge will carry on forever."

The method of instruction in the Faithkeeper's School has been called "natural and realistic." For instance, the children learn biology by studying nature. They learn anatomy by gutting a deer that has been brought in from the hunt. Other academic subjects are presently taught to the children by their parents at home. The children then complete these lessons the next day at school, assisted by Faithkeeper teachers. Because the school is not certified by the state, students who want a state-recognized diploma also attend the Salamanca public school.

It is of great concern to the Seneca elders that all their children should have the best education possible. In keeping with this hope for the future of their people, the Seneca Nation has obtained federal funding to provide workshops on pedagogy to help all teachers of Seneca children, including the Faith- keeper's teachers.

The Mohawks also continued their efforts to improve their educational facilities and increase their knowledge of their history and culture. There is a Freedom School at Akwesasne (St. Regis) that teaches Mohawk language by means of total immersion in the language. Also, in order to learn more of their own story over the years, the Mohawks persuaded a history professor at nearby St. Lawrence University to teach a course on the founding and development of Akwesasne and its current concerns. The university approved the course the professor prepared and granted it college credit. It was taught one evening a week for three hours each night in the spring of 2003 on the Akwesasne Reservation and had twenty Mohawk students and ten university students registered. The experience of this course has encouraged the Mohawks to seek to have an Akwesasne history book written.

Museums are another medium to educate people and preserve history and culture. Several Iroquois groups presently have fine museums, some of them with research facilities. The Woodland Indian Cultural Centre Museum is located at the Six Nations Reserve in Ontario, Canada. The Oneida Tribal Museum is on the Oneida Reservation in Wisconsin. The Seneca-Iroquois National Museum is located in Allegany Territory, Salamanca, New York. The Akwesasne Museum is at St. Regis. All were established by the Iroquois people of the nations concerned.

Through their many struggles to protect their treaty rights, their sovereignty, and their dignity, the Iroquois themselves have become educators to non-Indians. Not only have they been successful in bringing about improvements in their own reservation schools and environment, but they have also worked independently and with the New York State Education Department in requesting that non-Indian schools cease using Indian mascots as school symbols.

To some non-Indians, this request has often been puzzling, since they had not thought of their mascot symbols as offensive, particularly if the mascot is an Indian warrior who symbolizes their athletic teams. Indians, however, do not want themselves or their race appropriated as mascots for non-Indian schools, especially when the supposed Indian warrior acts as a clownish figure during athletic events. They feel it is demeaning for a human being to be used as a mascot. It is particularly offensive when, as sometimes happens, the mascot is a grinning cartoon Indian with a mouth full of oversized teeth.

St. John's University in New York City, acceded to Indian requests to change its symbol. The university's athletes used to be called "The Redmen." They are now known as "The Red Storm."

St. Bonaventure University, just a few miles east of Seneca Allegany territory, took more persuading. The university had as its mascot "The Brown Indian and the Squaw." Although the students and alumni were very attached to the symbol, the Senecas were offended by it, considering it to be racially insensitive. All Indians view the term *squaw* for "woman" as an insult. The Education Department of the Seneca Nation spoke on different occasions to the administration, alumni, and individual classes at St. Bonaventure to explain the problem. Finally, the university abandoned its old mascot and became instead "The Wolverines" in 1997.

The Native American Education Unit of the New York State Education Department has worked closely with State Education Commissioner Richard P. Mills to bring the problem of Indian mascots to the attention of New York State schools. On April 5, 2001, Commissioner Mills sent memos to all school districts in the state, asking for information on their mascots and whether they were offensive. To some schools, the matter of mascot change was an emotional, school loyalty issue rather than a financial problem. To others, it was definitely financial if they would have to spend thousands of dollars buying new uniforms for their sports teams. On June 5, 2002, Commissioner Mills sent out another memo, inquiring what the schools had done about their mascots such as Redskins, Braves, Indians, Warriors, and Redmen. About 23 percent announced that they had discontinued use of their offending mascot right away and had chosen another; 31 percent were still considering whether to change; and 42 percent, or 48 districts, had retained their Indian mascots. There was no response from a few districts. Some districts explained that their "Warriors" were not Indians but Romans or Trojans.

The Salamanca School District, which is located in the largely non-Indian city of Salamanca in Allegany Seneca territory, had "Salamanca Warriors" as its symbol. The situation was rather unique, since most Seneca children at Allegany attend the Salamanca schools. The warrior symbol, which had been drawn by a Seneca artist and inlaid on the gym floor, was a dignified depiction of a Seneca man wearing the traditional Iroquois

New York State Education Commissioner Richard P. Mills has worked closely with the Native American Education Unit of the New York State Education Department in attempting to protect the dignity of the Iroquois. In 1998, he launched a study to determine whether the use of American Indian mascots by New York's schools is offensive and should be abandoned.

headgear, or *gustoweh*. The overwhelming percentage of those Senecas surveyed on the issue found the symbol not offensive but rather an honor to Indians. It has accordingly been retained.

In addition to protecting the dignity of their people, the Iroquois seek to protect and preserve relics of their past. The repatriation of wampum kept in museums and also certain Iroquois religious articles also in museum collections has been an ongoing concern of confederacy people. The Onondagas, as the wampum keepers of the confederacy, have taken a leading role in attempting to retrieve the wampum that was once held by their nation. By 1971, the New York State legislature passed a bill permitting the return of only five of the eleven wampum belts kept in the New York State Museum if the Onondagas would build a suitable museum to house them. Governor Nelson Rockefeller then signed the bill. To the Onondagas, the terms were unacceptable. It would not be until 1989 that an agreement was reached and the eleven belts that had originally been acquired from Onondaga and an additional Iroquois belt were finally returned from the New York State Museum to the confederacy at Onondaga.

One of the returned wampum belts was known as the Hiawatha Belt. Against a background of purple beads it has five white beaded figures, representing the five original nations of the Iroquois Confederacy. The central figure, indicating the location of the Onondaga, is a white pine tree, the Tree of Peace, the symbol of the Iroquois Confederacy. The pattern of this Hiawatha Belt has now been adopted by the confederacy Iroquois as their national flag.

The year before the return of the wampum to the Iroquois Confederacy in New York, the Six Nations Reserve in Ontario, Canada, received eleven wampum belts that for years had been housed in the Heye Foundation Museum of the American Indian in New York City. These belts had been repatriated as a result of the demand of the chiefs at the Six Nations Reserve and the desire of the museum to retain the goodwill of the Iroquois. The belts were received on May 6, 1988, at a formal ceremony at the Onondaga Longhouse on the Six Nations Reserve, with the Indian recipients dressed in traditional

Iroquois ceremonial regalia for the important occasion. In 1999, an Iroquois repatriation committee retrieved more than four hundred religious ceremonial masks from the Heye Museum and returned them to the Iroquois communities in New York and Canada.

Another issue that has been important for Iroquois people is that of securing income for their communities. Some have sought to enhance their economies by establishing bingo operations on their reservations. More recently, there has also been an interest in casinos and the income they could generate.

By the early 1980s, Oneida Bingo was well under way among the Wisconsin Oneidas and proved to be very profitable to their nation. The tribe opened a hotel-restaurant to accommodate players who came from as far away as Chicago, Minneapolis, and Detroit. There are various other tribal businesses, such as stores, a gas station, and a cannery. Income from these operations, and primarily from bingo, has enabled the Oneidas to build a nursing home, a health-care facility, which includes a pharmacy, a day-care center, a library, a museum, a maintenance garage, and other enterprises, including housing, for their people.

The Seneca Nation in New York also has bingo but on a smaller scale than the system run by the Oneidas in Wisconsin. The Seneca-Cayuga Nation of Oklahoma operates a high-stakes bingo facility.

At St. Regis, there have been pro- and antibingo factions and the feelings sometimes have become very intense, causing the unity achieved in opposing the Seaway Authority to break down. In 1988, Congress passed the Indian Gaming Regulatory Act, which permitted casinos in Indian sovereign territory and gave states the privilege of negotiating gaming contracts with interested tribes. In 1990, a Mohawk individual at St. Regis opened an illegal casino without negotiating a contract with the state of New York and against the sentiment of a significant portion of the Mohawk Nation. The result was another division in the community and ongoing turmoil, including arrests by the state police, until the operation was finally shut down.

The first legal casino in New York State was Turning Stone, established at Oneida in 1993. St. Regis also legally opened a casino on its reservation in 1999.

Because of the dismal economic situation in western New York, Governor George Pataki and the state legislature negotiated with the Seneca Nation, allowing it to establish three casinos in the western part of the state in an effort to revive the economy. The state would also receive a percentage of the casino income from the Senecas. Originally, it was hoped that the first two casinos would be in Niagara Falls and Buffalo, both of which had lost industries and had high unemployment rates.

The Seneca Nation obtained the former Niagara Falls Convention Center and its fifty-five acres of land for its casino operation. Because casino gambling is illegal in New York except on Indian reservations, which are considered sovereign territory, the land on which the casino will operate was transferred to the Senecas as sovereign Indian land. Seneca Niagara Casino officially opened on December 31, 2002.

In late 2003, the Seneca Nation voted to establish its second casino on the Allegany Reservation in southern New York. Construction began immediately, with the opening scheduled to take place in mid-2004.

Not all Iroquois people welcome gaming into their communities. The Tuscarora Nation in western New York rejected bingo on its reservation in 1987 and, by massive protest demonstrations, shut down a nonapproved bingo hall before it could even open. The Onondagas, a conservative nation where there are many followers of the traditional Longhouse Religion, also disapproved of gambling and refused to have a casino in their community.

The so-called "bingo wars" and turbulence over proposed gaming operations at St. Regis in the late 1980s and early

1990s moved a small group of conservative and traditional Mohawks, led by Tom Porter, to seek a quieter location. They journeyed to the Mohawk River area, the historic homeland of their ancestors, and found a large, peaceful estate for sale near the little village of Fonda. With money they had made from the sale of their crafts and agricultural products, plus a large contribution from an anonymous donor, they were able to purchase the 322-acre estate in September 1993 and eventually turn it into a profitable farm and bed-and-breakfast establishment, with a craft shop, housing for community members, and conference rooms. Further land purchases have enlarged the estate to 403 acres.

They have named their operation *Kanatsiohareke* ("Place of the Clean Pot") after a nearby geological formation. This name is a modern Akwesasne rendering of the name of the old upper Mohawk village of *Canajoharie* ("Washed Kettle").

During the summer months, this establishment also functions as a language immersion school, attracting numbers of Iroquois people, mostly adults, from both reservations and urban areas, to participate in three-week-long sessions to increase their knowledge of their native language. Periodically, the bed and breakfast is closed down and the Mohawks hold a retreat session for Longhouse Religion adherents, with recitals of major rituals. Alcohol and drugs are strictly prohibited.

In a letter written to Tom Porter in December 1997, the Mohawk Nation Council of Chiefs said: "It is our pleasure to offer our full support for the educational endeavours you and the Community of Kanatsiohareke are pursuing. It has been a struggle to reverse the assimilation process that has been instituted by well-intentioned people of the United States and Canada. . . . We believe that a strong Mohawk language project partnered with Haudenosaunee philosophy and principles will do much to reverse the genocide of our culture . . . we would like to propose any assistance possible to promote the educational plans of Kanatsiohareke."

One of the major modern developments among the people of the Iroquois Confederacy in both Canada and New York has been the emergence of the environmental movement. Traditionally, Iroquois ancestors had always lived close to nature and were continually thankful to the Creator for the great gifts that were provided for their sustenance. The modern awakening of Iroquois people to environmental consciousness came as a result of the 1992 United Nations Earth Summit in Rio de Janeiro, Brazil. An Iroquois delegation was sent to the summit, as members later described their mission, "to spread the words of the Thanksgiving Address, the philosophy of our people." Upon their return home, a grand council was called by the confederacy chiefs to discuss the growing threat to the Iroquois environment. The result was the establishment of the Haudenosaunee Environmental Task Force (HETF).

The term *Haudenosaunee* comes from ethnologist Lewis Henry Morgan's transcription of the Seneca version of *Ongwano-sionni* ("We Are of the Extended Lodge"), the poetic Iroquois name for their confederacy. The Mohawks called it *Kanonghsionni*.

The goals of the Task Force were to restore environmental health in the Iroquois territories, improve communications among all the communities, inform the people about pollution issues and encourage activities preventing local pollution, sponsor ongoing community education on the environment, improve the skills of Iroquois people in conducting scientific research and testing for toxicants, protect the natural world, and develop programs that are culturally based to help preserve the environment for all Iroquois people.

Jim Ransom was chosen as HETF director and Dave Arquette as assistant director. To complete the team, Joyce King was chosen as cultural researcher and Barbara Gray as environmental law researcher. Each separate Iroquois reservation community in Canada and New York had its own director and staff for the HETF program, chosen by leaders of the local community. All are well-trained personnel.

Much care, education, and technical training go into developing staff to run the environmental programs for the Iroquois people. One example of the serious commitment of the environmental workers can be seen in the background of the director of the Tuscarora Environmental Program, Neil Patterson, Jr. Already interested in environmental concerns during his senior year in high school, he decided to attend an environmental college and chose the State University of New York Environmental Science and Forestry College at Syracuse University. During the summer after his graduation from high school, he became attracted to the work of HETF and was encouraged by some of the men of the community. He later traveled with HETF to discuss environmental concerns at other Iroquois communities. In addition, he assisted with work relating to the HETF report that was to be submitted at the United Nations Indigenous Summit in 1995. After his graduation from college, Patterson interned at the Environmental Protection Agency (EPA) in Washington, D.C., and later worked for a nonprofit environmental firm in Syracuse, New York.

As director of the Tuscarora Environmental Program, Patterson works closely with the chiefs and clanmothers and the members of the general Tuscarora community, both to give information and to receive advice and answer questions. He also oversees the training of interns and technicians and edits an environmental newsletter for the Tuscaroras.

Funding for each nation's environmental program may come from private sources, nonprofit agencies, or from HETF. The EPA and some other government agencies fund some of HETF's projects.

In addition to on-the-job training for interns and technicians, there are other agencies that help train personnel in environmental matters. One of the Tuscarora technicians, for instance, has received training at an air quality workshop at Northern Arizona University's Institute for Tribal Environmental Professionals, and at the Cortina Indian Rancheria of Wintun

Indians in California at an internship on the development of an emissions inventory, also sponsored by the Institute for Tribal Environmental Professionals.

In addition to local environmental matters involving members of their communities, two major issues confronted the Akwesasne Mohawks and the Tuscaroras at the beginning of the twenty-first century. The St. Lawrence–FDR Power Project license was about to expire in 2003 and was up for renewal. Environmental studies were necessary to renew the license. Akwesasne environmental groups were busy conducting a Culture Resource Study to investigate the impact on the local Mohawk environment of the St. Lawrence Seaway Project. The New York State Power Authority was likewise concerned about making compromises to satisfy both the inhabitants of the nearby non-Indian communities and the Mohawks so that it could receive its new license for the power project without ongoing objections and land claims that would complicate the renewal process.

The federal relicensing of the Niagara Power Project will be due in 2007, and this event impacts the Tuscarora Nation. Since the year 2000, the Tuscaroras and their Environmental Program have been involved in generating environmental studies both on the reservation and in the surrounding countryside to determine the environmental influence of the power project. These studies are required by the federal government before the power project can receive a new license. In addition, there must be a socioeconomic study and a historic properties and cultural resources study as well as a recreational resources study. The Tuscarora Nation expects to be very much involved in providing information for these studies and has already begun to collect and evaluate the required data.

The Iroquois are a resourceful people. They have endured for more than five centuries. In their past, they have known power and success and they have known misfortune. Throughout much of their recent history, they have experienced adversity but they have maintained an inner strength and a dignity that has made them determined never to be defeated. They have a strong attachment to their own history and culture and they have adopted techniques of the modern world to ensure their survival as a people far into the coming centuries.

The Iroquois at a Glance

Tribes	Mohawk, Oneida, Onondaga, Cayuga, Seneca, Tuscarora
Culture Area	Northeast
Original Geography	Upstate New York, south of Lake Ontario
Present Reservations	New York State, Quebec, Ontario, Wisconsin, Oklahoma
Linguistic Family	Iroquoian
Current Population (2000)	About 81,000
First European Contact	Jacques Cartier, French, 1534, St. Lawrence Iroquois groups; Samuel de Champlain, French, 1609, New York Iroquois
Federal Status	Recognized

c. 1459   Founding of the Iroquois Confederacy, according to nineteenth-century scholar Horatio Hale.

1534   Jacques Cartier leads a group of French explorers along St. Lawrence River.

1609   Raids by Mohawks and other tribes on European settlements along St. Lawrence River; Samuel de Champlain and his French troops defeat a group of Iroquois in a battle near the southern end of what is now Lake Champlain.

1610   On June 19, the French and some Indian allies defeat the Iroquois in the Battle of the Richelieu.

1626   The Mohawks defeat a Dutch-Mahican war party that had invaded their territory.

1630s–1640s   The Mohawks attempt to establish peace agreements with their various enemies.

1643   The Mohawks sign a treaty of alliance with the Dutch.

1645   The Mohawks sign a peace treaty with the French and France's Algonquin and Huron allies.

1647   The Huron Nation convinces the Oneida, Cayuga, and Onondaga tribes to agree to a truce in their ongoing war.

1648   The Dutch officially adopt a policy of selling arms to the Mohawks; on July 3, the Senecas attack a Jesuit missionary community in which many Huron people live.

1649   On March 16, the Iroquois attack and overtake the Huron village of Taenhatentaron; on March 17, the Iroquois army moves toward Sainte-Marie and is driven back by the Hurons; nonetheless, the battles of 1649 forever destroy the power of the Hurons.

1651   Seneca army invades Neutral lands and are ultimately driven away by the Neutrals.

1653   Oneida, Seneca, Cayuga, and Onondaga tribes establish peace with the French colonists living along the St. Lawrence River.

1654 Mohawks express their displeasure that the French are dealing primarily with the Onondagas, rather than with the Mohawks, who are known as the Keepers of the Eastern Door and are traditionally the first to deal with foreign visitors.

1664 English conquer New Netherland and rename it New York; French decide to try to stop any further Iroquois aggression.

1666 French invade Mohawk territory.

1667–1668 A group of Oneidas takes up residence near Montreal.

1674 Edmund Andros, the new governor of New York, tries to strengthen English alliances with Algonkian and Iroquois groups.

1680 Iroquois begin a series of wars against the Indian allies of the French.

1687 Governor of New France Jacques-René de Brisay Denonville invades and destroys Seneca villages.

1689–1697 King William's War is fought between France and England.

1699 New York revokes fraudulent land claims made by Godfrey Dellius after the Iroquois leader Hendrick makes his case against Dellius.

1700 Iroquois make efforts to establish peace with the French.

1701 Peace policy between the Iroquois and French goes into effect in August.

1702–1713 Queen Anne's War is fought between the French and British; after the wars of 1710–1713, the Tuscarora Nation migrates north to Pennsylvania and New York to be under the protection of the Extended Lodge.

1744–1748 King George's War is fought between the French and British.

1749 Sulpician missionary Abbé François Picquet sets up mission called La Presentation.

c. 1750 A group of Caughnawagas settles near French mission of St. Regis.

1754–1763 French and Indian War (called the Seven Years' War in Europe) is fought between the French and British.

1755 Hendrick Peters leads a group of warriors into battle against the French; although the British and Iroquois troops are victorious, Hendrick is killed in battle.

1763–1764 Pontiac's Conspiracy, an Indian rebellion against the English, takes place; it fails to oust the English and results in the loss of more Indian territory.

1779 General George Washington authorizes an invasion of Iroquois country.

1783 Treaty of Paris ends the American Revolution after the British defeat.

1784 On October 22, the Continental Congress signs the Treaty of Fort Stanwix with the Loyalist Iroquois who had refused to acknowledge the American victory in the Revolution; the treaty brings peace to the Mohawk, Cayuga, Onondaga, Seneca, Oneida, and Tuscarora tribes; on October 23, the Indian delegates to the treaty conference sign away another large tract of land.

1790 U.S. Nonintercourse Act (followed by a similar act in 1793) forbids purchases of Indian lands without a U.S. commissioner present at the sale.

1794 Treaty of Canandaigua guarantees the Senecas possession of their lands forever.

1798 Quakers send teachers and workers to help improve the lives of the Senecas living along the New York–Pennsylvania border.

1799 Handsome Lake has a spiritual vision and begins to create his Longhouse Religion.

1802 The Mohawks living on the U.S. side of the border adopt an elective system of government.

c. 1806 Oswegatchie settlement is abandoned.

1830–1846 U.S. policy attempts to force all eastern Indians to move west of the Mississippi River to make room for additional white settlement.

1831 Because of the U.S. removal policy, the Iroquois of Ohio sell off their reservations at Lewistown and Sandusky and move to Indian Territory.

1838 Ogden Land Company negotiates the fraudulent Treaty of Buffalo Creek, depriving the Senecas of all their remaining reservations.

1842 The Allegany and Cattaraugus reservations are returned to the Senecas.

1848 The Senecas living on the Allegany and Cattaraugus reservations carry out a nonviolent revolution, overthrowing the chiefs with whose rule they have become dissatisfied.

1857 Tonawanda Senecas repurchase most of their reservation from the Ogden Land Company.

1887 General Allotment Act tries to break up Indian reservations by granting individuals smaller parcels of land.

1920s Longhouse Religion established on the Caughnawaga Reservation.

1924 An elective council is established on the Six Nations Reserve; Immigration Act of 1924, put into place to keep out Asians from the United States, has the effect of banning Indians from crossing the Canadian–United States border.

1926 Indian Defense League of America formed.

1928 Courts specifically reaffirm the right of Indians to freely cross the U.S.-Canadian border.

1930s Longhouse Religion established on the St. Regis Reservation.

1934 Indian Reorganization Act allows tribes some self-government on reservations; Wisconsin Oneidas create a new government and write a constitution.

1940s–1950s U.S. government tries to end its involvement in Indian affairs by "terminating" tribal status and encouraging Indians to move off reservations and into urban areas.

1942 Seneca Nation wins a lawsuit in the U.S. Court of Appeals for the Second Circuit of New York against non-Indian leaseholders on the Allegany Reservation.

1958–1960 Tuscaroras fight an attempt by the New York State Power Authority to take over a large portion of their reservation to create a reservoir; on March 7, 1960, the U.S. Supreme Court decides against the Tuscaroras.

1959 Hereditary chiefs at Six Nations Reserve try and fail to overthrow the reservation government; Mohawk Chief John Sharrow demands $45,000 in rent money from the St. Lawrence Seaway Authority; the Authority pays the requested sum.

1964 Women of the Seneca Nation receive the right to vote.

1966 Oneida Robert L. Bennett is appointed commissioner of Indian Affairs.

1968 Mohawks on Cornwall Island are told they will have to pay customs duties on any purchased items brought to the island; on December 18, the Mohawks stage a blockade of the International Bridge to protest the customs policy; North American Indian Travelling College is established; Mohawks at St. Regis stage a boycott of the Salmon River School District to protest the inadequate attention being paid to Indian children.

1969 The Mohawks stage another blockade of the International Bridge, and the Canadian government agrees not to levy the customs duties.

1970 Once again, the hereditary chiefs at Six Nations Reserve try and fail to oust the reservation government.

1971 Onondagas withdraw their children from the Lafayette School District in protest of their treatment.

1974   U.S. Supreme Court gives the Oneidas of New York access to federal courts to pursue their land claims cases.

1985   Oneidas win a test case in the U.S. Supreme Court for illegal seizure of their lands in what became Oneida and Madison counties.

1987   Tuscarora Nation rejects bingo on its reservation.

1988   U.S. Congress passes the Indian Gaming Regulatory Act, allowing for casino gambling on Indian reservations.

1989   New York State Museum returns contested wampum belts to the Iroquois Confederacy.

1990   A Mohawk opens an illegal casino at St. Regis.

1993   The Oneidas open Turning Stone, the first legal casino in New York State; Tom Porter and other conservative Mohawks establish Kanatsiohareke, a bed and breakfast and educational center.

1997   St. Bonaventure University changes its mascot from "The Brown Indian and the Squaw" to "The Wolverines."

1999   An Iroquois repatriation committee retrieves more than four hundred religious ceremonial masks from the Heye Museum; St. Regis Reservation opens a legal casino.

2000   Faithkeepers' School is founded at Allegany Reservation.

2001   After a jury decided in a 2000 case that lands taken from the Cayugas were worth $37.8 million, a judge rules that the Cayuga Nation of New York and the Seneca-Cayuga Tribe of Oklahoma are due an additional $211 million.

2002   Seneca Niagara Casino opens.

2003   Seneca Nation votes to open a second casino on the Allegany Reservation in southern New York.

Algonkian—The Indian people living in the northeastern United States and east-central Canada whose languages are related and who share numerous cultural characteristics.

Algonquian—The languages spoken by most Indian peoples in northeastern North America, including those who geographically surrounded the Iroquois.

Algonquins—A tribal group living in the Ottawa River valley region of Canada. In colonial times, they were an important ally of France.

anthropology—The study of the physical, social, and cultural characteristics of human beings.

blood feud—Violent acts of retaliation between individuals and families resulting in ongoing revenge.

clan—A group in American Indian society who traces its descent, either actually or theoretically, from a common ancestor. Membership in a clan establishes membership in a tribe. Among the Iroquois, descent and consequently clan membership are traced through the mother's line only.

culture—The total learned behavior and ways of thinking of human beings; the socially transmitted, nonbiological activities that constitute the way of life of a given group of people.

culture area—A geographical region in which the cultures of a number of tribes or other groups share numerous traits or elements.

exorcism—The process of driving out or expelling an evil spirit from an afflicted individual.

Iroquoian—A large group of separate tribal peoples in the Northeast and Carolina regions speaking related languages and having similar cultures. Most were eventually conquered or incorporated by the Six Nations. Also, the languages spoken by these tribal groups.

Iroquois—The Iroquoian people; specifically, the Six Nations: Mohawk, Oneida, Onondaga, Cayuga, Seneca, and Tuscarora.

Jesuit—A member of the Society of Jesus, a Roman Catholic religious order founded by Ignatius Loyola in 1534. The Jesuits were highly learned and active in spreading the faith.

lineage—A group of individuals related through descent from a common ancestor; a descent group whose members recognize as relatives people on the mother's side only or the father's side only.

matchlock—An old form of portable firearm having a burning wick (match) for firing the priming powder.

matrilineal descent—Relationship traced through the mother's line.

nation—A term used generally by the early Europeans in North America to describe the Indian tribal societies they encountered. Broadly, any large group of people having similar institutions, language, customs, and political and social ties.

ohwachira—A basic political and social unit in the Iroquois clan comprising all the male and female children of a leading woman and all the descendants of her female children. One or more *ohwachiras* constituted a clan. Certain *ohwachiras* within a clan held the right to chiefship titles.

patrilineal descent—Relationship traced through the father's line.

Quakers—The familiar name for members of the Religious Society of Friends, a mystical and pacifist group founded in England by George Fox in the seventeenth century. Quakers were active in efforts to help Indians during the nineteenth century.

relocation—The attempt on the part of the federal government to encourage Indians to leave the tribal environment of the reservation and migrate to cities in order to enter mainstream society.

reservation—Indian homelands either set aside by the U.S. or Canadian government or retained by Indians as a result of past treaty negotiations; land designated for occupation by and for the use of Indians. In Canada, they are usually called *reserves*.

sachem—A tribal ruler or chief. The word comes from the Narragansett dialect of New England and was applied by Europeans to chiefs of non-Iroquois tribes in the Northeast. When applied to the Iroquois, it refers to the hereditary civil or peace chiefs, the "lords" of the confederacy.

shaman—A person who has special powers to call on spirit beings and mediate between the supernatural world and the world of ordinary people. The word comes from the Tungus language of Siberia.

squatters—People who occupy and live on a plot of land without having legal title to it.

state—A form of social and political organization embracing a territory and having laws supported by force and sanctions. People in a state society are divided into social and economic classes, privileged and subordinate groups.

termination—The removal of Indian tribes from federal government supervision and Indian lands from federal trust status. The policy was initiated by Congress during the presidencies of Harry Truman and Dwight Eisenhower.

tribe—A type of society consisting of several or many separate communities bound together by common language, territory, and culture. A tribe's communities are united by kinship and such social units as clans, religious organizations, and economic and political institutions. They generally lack a centralized government that can enforce political decisions.

wampum—Shell beads used by the Iroquois in strings or "belts" as a pledge of the truth of their words, symbols of high office, records of diplomatic negotiations and treaties, and records of other important events. From the Algonquian word *wampumpeag*, meaning "white (bead) strings."

witchcraft—The practice of doing harm to others by use of black, or evil, magic.

Books

Akwesasne Notes (editor). *A Basic Call to Consciousness.* Summertown, Tenn.: Book Publishing Company, 1992.

Armstrong, William H. *Warrior in Two Camps: Ely S. Parker, Union General and Seneca Chief.* Syracuse, N.Y.: Syracuse University Press, 1978.

Cornplanter, Jesse J. *Legends of the Longhouse.* New York: Ira J. Friedman, 1963.

Densmore, Christopher. *Red Jacket: Iroquois Diplomat and Orator.* Syracuse, N.Y.: Syracuse University Press, 1999.

Fenton, William N. *The False Faces of the Iroquois.* Norman, Okla.: University of Oklahoma Press, 1987.

George-Kanentiio, Doug. *Iroquois Culture and Commentary.* Santa Fe, N.M.: Clear Light Publishers, 2000.

Graymont, Barbara. *The Iroquois in the American Revolution.* Syracuse, N.Y.: Syracuse University Press, 1972.

Hale, Horatio, ed. *The Iroquois Book of Rites.* Toronto: University of Toronto Press, 1963.

Hauptman, Laurence M. *The Iroquois Struggle for Survival: World War II to Red Power.* Syracuse, N.Y.: Syracuse University Press, 1986.

Jemison, Mary. *The Narrative Life of Mary Jemison.* Syracuse, N.Y.: Syracuse University Press, 1990.

Jennings, Francis. *The Ambiguous Iroquois Empire.* New York: W.W. Norton & Company, 1990.

Kelsay, Isabel Thompson. *Joseph Brant, 1743–1807: Man of Two Worlds.* Syracuse, N.Y.: Syracuse University Press, 1984.

Morgan, Lewis H. *League of the Iroquois.* New York: Corinth Books, 1962.

Parker, Arthur C. *Parker on the Iroquois,* ed. William N. Fenton. Syracuse, N.Y.: Syracuse University Press, 1968.

Richter, Daniel K. *The Ordeal of the Longhouse: The Peoples of the Iroquois League in the Era of European Colonization.* Omohundro Institute of Early American History. Chapel Hill, N.C.: University of North Carolina Press, 1993.

Rickard, Clinton. *Fighting Tuscarora: The Autobiography of Chief Clinton Rickard*, ed. Barbara Graymont. Syracuse, N.Y.: Syracuse University Press, 1973.

Tooker, Elisabeth. *Lewis H. Morgan on Iroquois Material Culture*. Tucson, Ariz.: University of Arizona Press, 1994.

Wallace, Anthony F. C. *The Death and Rebirth of the Seneca*. New York: Knopf, 1970.

———. "Dreams and Wishes of the Soul; A Type of Psychoanalytic Theory Among the Seventeenth Century Iroquois." *American Anthropologist* 60 (March 1958): 234–248.

Wallace, Paul. *White Roots of Peace: Iroquois Book of Life*. Santa Fe, N.M.: Clear Light Publishers, 1998.

Wallace, Paul A. W. *The White Roots of Peace*. New York: Ira J. Friedman, 1968.

Websites

Haudenosaunee Environmental Task Force (HETF)
http://www.hetfonline.org

The Iroquois Constitution (at the University of Oklahoma Law Center)
http://www.law.ou.edu/hist/iroquois.html

Iroquois Indian Museum
http://www.iroquoismuseum.org

Iroquois Information Links
http://tuscaroras.com/pages/irlinks_na.html

Iroquois Language and Songs
http://collections.ic.gc.ca/language

Iroquois Net
http://www.iroquois.net

Oneida Nation of Wisconsin
http://www.oneidanation.org

Seneca-Iroquois National Museum
http://www.senecamuseum.org

Seneca Nation of Indians
http://www.sni.org

PICTURE CREDITS

Barbara Graymont, a historian and leading authority on the Iroquois Indians, received a Ph.D. in history from Columbia University. She is professor emerita of history at Nyack College, Nyack, New York, and previously taught at Bates College, Lewiston, Maine. Dr. Graymont is the author of numerous books and articles, including several volumes in the series EARLY AMERICAN INDIAN DOCUMENTS. Her book *The Iroquois in the American Revolution* was cited as a source in a 1985 U.S. Supreme Court decision that upheld a land claim of the Oneida Indian Nation. For many years, she has spent summers living and working among the Tuscarora Indians of Upstate New York, researching and writing about their history and culture. She has been involved in Indian rights movements and is an honorary member of the Indian Defense League of America.

Ada E. Deer is the director of the American Indian Studies program at the University of Wisconsin-Madison. She was the first woman to serve as chair of her tribe, the Menominee Nation, the first woman to head the Bureau of Indian Affairs in the U.S. Department of the Interior, and the first American Indian woman to run for Congress and secretary of state of Wisconsin. Deer has also chaired the Native American Rights Fund, coordinated workshops to train American Indian women as leaders, and championed Indian participation in the Peace Corps. She holds degrees in social work from Wisconsin and Columbia.